The Nation's #1 Educational Publisher

The McGraw·Hill Companies

P9-CAN-585

Grade 1

Addition • Subtraction
Measurement • Time • Money

A McGraw·Hill/Warner Bros. Workbook

Table of Contents

Table of Contents (continued)

Credits:
McGraw-Hill Learning Materials Editorial/Production Team
Vincent F. Douglas, B.S. and M. Ed.
Tracy R. Paulus
Jennifer P. Blashkiw

Design Studio
Mike Legendre; Creativity On Demand

Warner Bros. Worldwide Publishing Editorial/Production Team
Michael Harkavy   Charles Carney
Paula Allen   Allen Helbig
Victoria Selover   Sara Hunter

Illustrators
Cover and Interior: Animated Arts!™

McGraw-Hill
Consumer Products

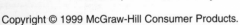

A Division of The McGraw-Hill Companies

Send all inquiries to:
McGraw-Hill Consumer Products
250 Old Wilson Bridge Road
Worthington, Ohio 43085

1-57768-201-7

NUMBERS 0 TO 3

zero	one	two	three
0	1	2	3

Circle the number.

0   1   (2)   3

0   1   2   3

0   1   2   3

0   1   2   3

0   1   2   3

0   1   2   3

3

NUMBERS 4 TO 7

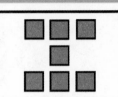

  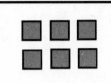 

four	five	six	seven
4	5	6	7

Circle the number.

4   (5)   6   7

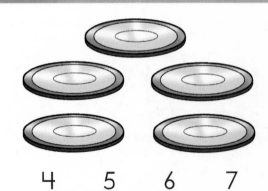

4   5   6   7

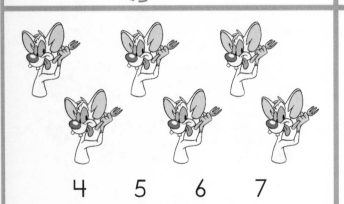

4   5   6   7

4   5   6   7

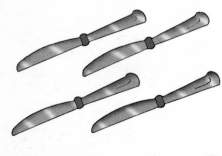

4   5   6   7

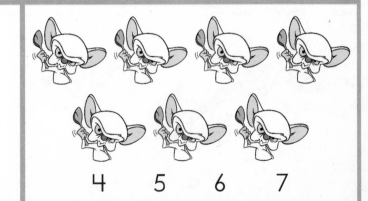

4   5   6   7

4

NUMBERS 8 TO 10

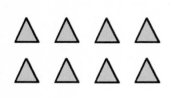

eight	nine	ten
8	9	10

Circle the number.

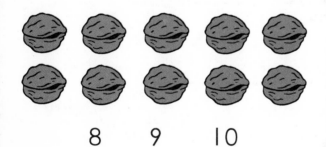

8   9   ⟨10⟩

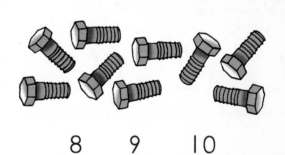

8   9   10

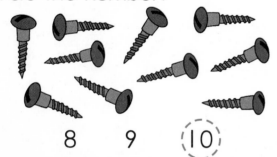

8   9   10

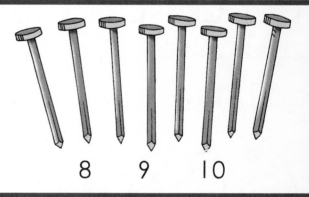

8   9   10

8   9   10

8   9   10

ORDER OF NUMBERS

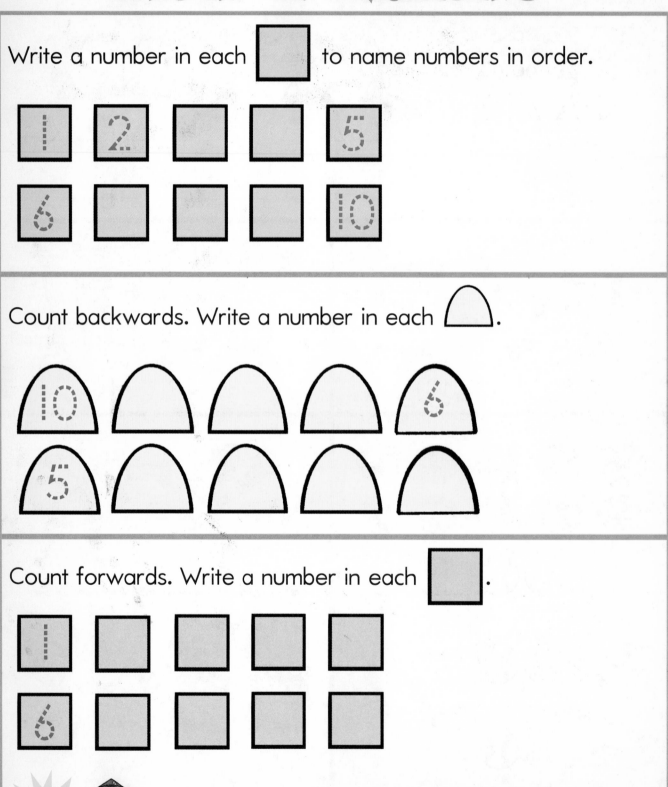

Write a number in each ▢ to name numbers in order.

| 1 | 2 | | | 5 |

| 6 | | | | 10 |

Count backwards. Write a number in each ⌓.

| 10 | | | | 6 |

| 5 | | | | |

Count forwards. Write a number in each ▢.

| 1 | | | | |

| 6 | | | | |

6

ORDER OF NUMBERS

Count forwards. Write the number in each ▷.

Then trace the number words on the - - - -.

▷ zero

⚾ ▷ one

⚾⚾ ▷ two

⚾⚾⚾ ▷ three

⚾⚾⚾⚾ ▷ four

⚾⚾⚾⚾⚾ ▷ five

⚾⚾⚾⚾⚾⚾ ▷ six

⚾⚾⚾⚾⚾⚾⚾ ▷ seven

ORDER OF NUMBERS

Connect the dots in order from 0 to 10.

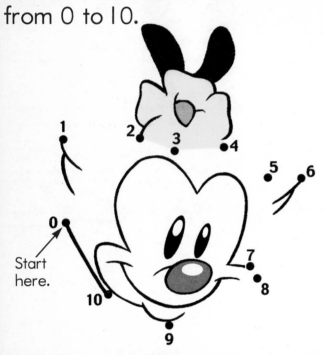

1
2
3
4
5
6
0
Start here.
7
8
10
9

Start here.
0
1
2
10
9
8
3
7
6
4
5

0
1
Start here.
2
4
3
5
6
7
10
9
8

4
6
5
3
7
2
8
9
1
Start here.
0
10

CHECKUP

Tell how many.

(5 circles) _____	(7 squares) _____	(1 rectangle) _____
(9 diamonds) _____	_____	(5 rectangles) _____

Read the number. Draw that many X's.

7	4	3
10	2	8

9

SUMS THROUGH 3

Add.

$$\begin{array}{r} 1 \\ + 1 \\ \hline 2 \end{array}$$

$1 + 1 = 2$

$$\begin{array}{r} 2 \\ + 1 \\ \hline \end{array}$$

$2 + 1 =$

$$\begin{array}{r} 1 \\ + 2 \\ \hline \end{array}$$

$1 + 2 =$

$$\begin{array}{r} 2 \\ + 0 \\ \hline \end{array}$$

$2 + 0 =$

$$\begin{array}{r} 0 \\ + 2 \\ \hline \end{array}$$

$0 + 2 =$

$$\begin{array}{r} 3 \\ + 0 \\ \hline \end{array}$$

$3 + 0 =$

$$\begin{array}{r} 0 \\ + 3 \\ \hline \end{array}$$

$0 + 3 =$

$$\begin{array}{r} 0 \\ + 0 \\ \hline \end{array}$$

$0 + 0 =$

$$\begin{array}{r} 1 \\ + 0 \\ \hline \end{array}$$

$1 + 0 =$

$$\begin{array}{r} 0 \\ + 1 \\ \hline \end{array}$$

$0 + 1 =$

SUMS OF 4 AND 5

Add.

$\begin{array}{r} 4 \\ + 1 \\ \hline \end{array}$

$4 + 1 = 5$

$\begin{array}{r} 1 \\ + 4 \\ \hline \end{array}$

$1 + 4 =$

$\begin{array}{r} 2 \\ + 3 \\ \hline \end{array}$

$2 + 3 =$

$\begin{array}{r} 3 \\ + 2 \\ \hline \end{array}$

$3 + 2 =$

$\begin{array}{r} 2 \\ + 2 \\ \hline \end{array}$

$2 + 2 =$

$\begin{array}{r} 4 \\ + 0 \\ \hline \end{array}$

$4 + 0 =$

$\begin{array}{r} 0 \\ + 4 \\ \hline \end{array}$

$0 + 4 =$

$\begin{array}{r} 0 \\ + 5 \\ \hline \end{array}$

$0 + 5 =$

$\begin{array}{r} 5 \\ + 0 \\ \hline \end{array}$

$5 + 0 =$

$\begin{array}{r} 1 \\ + 3 \\ \hline \end{array}$

$1 + 3 =$

$\begin{array}{r} 3 \\ + 1 \\ \hline \end{array}$

$3 + 1 =$

SUBTRACTING FROM 1, 2, AND 3

Subtract.

$$\begin{array}{r} 3 \\ -\ 1 \\ \hline 2 \end{array}$$

3 − 1 = 2

$$\begin{array}{r} 2 \\ -\ 1 \\ \hline \end{array}$$

2 − 1 =

$$\begin{array}{r} 3 \\ -\ 2 \\ \hline \end{array}$$

3 − 2 =

$$\begin{array}{r} 1 \\ -\ 0 \\ \hline \end{array}$$

1 − 0 =

$$\begin{array}{r} 3 \\ -\ 0 \\ \hline \end{array}$$

3 − 0 =

$$\begin{array}{r} 1 \\ -\ 1 \\ \hline \end{array}$$

1 − 1 =

$$\begin{array}{r} 2 \\ -\ 2 \\ \hline \end{array}$$

2 − 2 =

$$\begin{array}{r} 3 \\ -\ 3 \\ \hline \end{array}$$

3 − 3 =

SUBTRACTING FROM 4 AND 5

Subtract.

$$\begin{array}{r} 5 \\ -1 \\ \hline 4 \end{array}$$

5 − 1 = 4

$$\begin{array}{r} 4 \\ -3 \\ \hline \end{array}$$

4 − 3 =

$$\begin{array}{r} 5 \\ -4 \\ \hline \end{array}$$

5 − 4 =

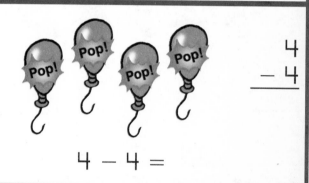
$$\begin{array}{r} 4 \\ -4 \\ \hline \end{array}$$

4 − 4 =

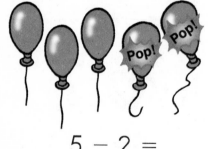
$$\begin{array}{r} 5 \\ -2 \\ \hline \end{array}$$

5 − 2 =

$$\begin{array}{r} 4 \\ -2 \\ \hline \end{array}$$

4 − 2 =

$$\begin{array}{r} 5 \\ -3 \\ \hline \end{array}$$

5 − 3 =

$$\begin{array}{r} 4 \\ -1 \\ \hline \end{array}$$

4 − 1 =

NUMBER FAMILIES

Add or subtract.

2	1	3	3
+ 1	+ 2	− 2	− 1
3	3	1	2

1	3	4	4
+ 3	+ 1	− 1	− 3

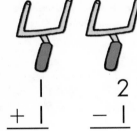

2	3	5	5
+ 3	+ 2	− 2	− 3

4	1	5	5
+ 1	+ 4	− 4	− 1

1	2
+ 1	− 1

2	4
+ 2	− 2

2	0	2	2
+ 0	+ 2	− 2	− 0

5	0	5	5
+ 0	+ 5	− 5	− 0

CHECKUP

Add.

3 + 1	1 + 1	0 + 0	2 + 1	5 + 0	1 + 0
0 + 3	2 + 2	1 + 2	0 + 1	1 + 4	3 + 2
1 + 3	4 + 0	0 + 5	2 + 0	4 + 1	2 + 3

Subtract.

2 − 1	4 − 1	5 − 0	3 − 2	5 − 4	4 − 4
4 − 0	5 − 1	0 − 0	4 − 2	3 − 0	5 − 2
2 − 0	4 − 3	5 − 3	3 − 1	3 − 3	1 − 1

SUMS OF 6

Add.

$\begin{array}{r} 1 \\ + 5 \\ \hline \end{array}$

1 + 5 = 6   6

$\begin{array}{r} 5 \\ + 1 \\ \hline \end{array}$

5 + 1 =

$\begin{array}{r} 2 \\ + 4 \\ \hline \end{array}$

2 + 4 =

$\begin{array}{r} 4 \\ + 2 \\ \hline \end{array}$

4 + 2 =

$\begin{array}{r} 6 \\ + 0 \\ \hline \end{array}$

6 + 0 =

$\begin{array}{r} 0 \\ + 6 \\ \hline \end{array}$

0 + 6 =

$\begin{array}{r} 3 \\ + 3 \\ \hline \end{array}$

3 + 3 =

$\begin{array}{r} 2 \\ + 4 \\ \hline \end{array}$ $\begin{array}{r} 1 \\ + 3 \\ \hline \end{array}$ $\begin{array}{r} 5 \\ + 1 \\ \hline \end{array}$ $\begin{array}{r} 3 \\ + 3 \\ \hline \end{array}$ $\begin{array}{r} 2 \\ + 2 \\ \hline \end{array}$ $\begin{array}{r} 3 \\ + 2 \\ \hline \end{array}$

SUBTRACTING FROM 6

Subtract.

$$\begin{array}{r} 6 \\ -\ 1 \\ \hline 5 \end{array}$$

$6 - 1 = 5$

$$\begin{array}{r} 6 \\ -\ 5 \\ \hline \end{array}$$

$6 - 5 =$

$$\begin{array}{r} 6 \\ -\ 4 \\ \hline \end{array}$$

$6 - 4 =$

$$\begin{array}{r} 6 \\ -\ 2 \\ \hline \end{array}$$

$6 - 2 =$

$$\begin{array}{r} 6 \\ -\ 3 \\ \hline \end{array}$$

$6 - 3 =$

$$\begin{array}{r} 6 \\ -\ 0 \\ \hline \end{array}$$

$6 - 0 =$

$$\begin{array}{r} 6 \\ -\ 3 \\ \hline \end{array} \qquad \begin{array}{r} 6 \\ -\ 6 \\ \hline \end{array} \qquad \begin{array}{r} 6 \\ -\ 1 \\ \hline \end{array} \qquad \begin{array}{r} 6 \\ -\ 4 \\ \hline \end{array} \qquad \begin{array}{r} 6 \\ -\ 2 \\ \hline \end{array} \qquad \begin{array}{r} 6 \\ -\ 5 \\ \hline \end{array}$$

Add.

$$\begin{array}{r} 3 \\ + 4 \\ \hline 7 \end{array}$$

3 + 4 = 7

$$\begin{array}{r} 6 \\ + 1 \\ \hline \end{array}$$

6 + 1 =

$$\begin{array}{r} 4 \\ + 3 \\ \hline \end{array}$$

4 + 3 =

$$\begin{array}{r} 1 \\ + 6 \\ \hline \end{array}$$

1 + 6 =

$$\begin{array}{r} 7 \\ + 0 \\ \hline \end{array}$$

7 + 0 =

$$\begin{array}{r} 2 \\ + 5 \\ \hline \end{array}$$

2 + 5 =

$$\begin{array}{r} 0 \\ + 7 \\ \hline \end{array}$$

0 + 7 =

$$\begin{array}{r} 5 \\ + 2 \\ \hline \end{array}$$

5 + 2 =

$$\begin{array}{r} 5 \\ + 2 \\ \hline \end{array}$$
$$\begin{array}{r} 3 \\ + 3 \\ \hline \end{array}$$
$$\begin{array}{r} 4 \\ + 3 \\ \hline \end{array}$$
$$\begin{array}{r} 1 \\ + 6 \\ \hline \end{array}$$
$$\begin{array}{r} 3 \\ + 4 \\ \hline \end{array}$$
$$\begin{array}{r} 6 \\ + 0 \\ \hline \end{array}$$

NAME _____

SUBTRACTING FROM 7

Subtract.

$$\begin{array}{r} 7 \\ -\ 6 \\ \hline \end{array}$$

$7 - 6 =$

$$\begin{array}{r} 7 \\ -\ 1 \\ \hline \end{array}$$

$7 - 1 =$

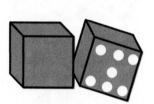

$$\begin{array}{r} 7 \\ -\ 3 \\ \hline \end{array}$$

$7 - 3 =$

$$\begin{array}{r} 7 \\ -\ 4 \\ \hline \end{array}$$

$7 - 4 =$

$$\begin{array}{r} 7 \\ -\ 7 \\ \hline \end{array}$$

$7 - 7 =$

$$\begin{array}{r} 7 \\ -\ 0 \\ \hline \end{array}$$

$7 - 0 =$

$$\begin{array}{r} 7 \\ -\ 2 \\ \hline \end{array}$$

$7 - 2 =$

$$\begin{array}{r} 7 \\ -\ 5 \\ \hline \end{array}$$

$7 - 5 =$

19

SUMS OF 8

Add.

$$\begin{array}{r} 5 \\ + 3 \\ \hline \end{array}$$

5 + 3 = **8**   **8**

$$\begin{array}{r} 7 \\ + 1 \\ \hline \end{array}$$

7 + 1 =

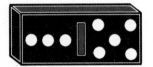

$$\begin{array}{r} 3 \\ + 5 \\ \hline \end{array}$$

3 + 5 =

$$\begin{array}{r} 1 \\ + 7 \\ \hline \end{array}$$

1 + 7 =

$$\begin{array}{r} 2 \\ + 6 \\ \hline \end{array}$$

2 + 6 =

$$\begin{array}{r} 4 \\ + 4 \\ \hline \end{array}$$

4 + 4 =

$$\begin{array}{r} 6 \\ + 2 \\ \hline \end{array}$$

6 + 2 =

$$\begin{array}{r} 3 \\ + 3 \\ \hline \end{array} \qquad \begin{array}{r} 5 \\ + 3 \\ \hline \end{array} \qquad \begin{array}{r} 2 \\ + 6 \\ \hline \end{array} \qquad \begin{array}{r} 8 \\ + 0 \\ \hline \end{array} \qquad \begin{array}{r} 4 \\ + 3 \\ \hline \end{array} \qquad \begin{array}{r} 0 \\ + 8 \\ \hline \end{array}$$

SUBTRACTING FROM 8

Subtract.

$$\begin{array}{r} 8 \\ -\ 7 \\ \hline \end{array}$$

8 − 7 =

$$\begin{array}{r} 8 \\ -\ 1 \\ \hline \end{array}$$

8 − 1 =

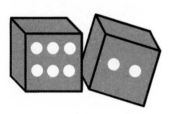

$$\begin{array}{r} 8 \\ -\ 2 \\ \hline \end{array}$$

8 − 2 =

$$\begin{array}{r} 8 \\ -\ 6 \\ \hline \end{array}$$

8 − 6 =

$$\begin{array}{r} 8 \\ -\ 4 \\ \hline \end{array}$$

8 − 4 =

$$\begin{array}{r} 8 \\ -\ 8 \\ \hline \end{array}$$

8 − 8 =

$$\begin{array}{r} 8 \\ -\ 3 \\ \hline \end{array}$$

8 − 3 =

$$\begin{array}{r} 8 \\ -\ 5 \\ \hline \end{array}$$

8 − 5 =

21

ADDITION AND SUBTRACTION

Add.

5	1	3	2	1	5
+ 3	+ 6	+ 3	+ 6	+ 7	+ 1

0	4	4	6	3	6
+ 7	+ 2	+ 4	+ 0	+ 4	+ 1

3	8	5	2	6	0
+ 5	+ 0	+ 2	+ 4	+ 2	+ 8

Subtract.

8	6	8	7	6	6
− 3	− 5	− 4	− 3	− 2	− 6

8	7	8	7	8	7
− 5	− 0	− 1	− 6	− 6	− 5

8	6	7	8	6	7
− 8	− 3	− 1	− 2	− 1	− 2

PROBLEM SOLVING

Solve each problem.

There are 6 blue 👕.

There are 2 white 👕.

How many in all?

$$\begin{array}{r} 6 \\ +\ 2 \\ \hline 8 \end{array}$$

There are 7 🐦.

4 🐦 fly away.

How many are left?

$$\begin{array}{r} 7 \\ -\ 4 \\ \hline \end{array}$$

I saw 2 big 🍭.

I saw 3 little 🍭.

How many in all?

$$\begin{array}{r} 2 \\ +\ 3 \\ \hline \end{array}$$

Pinky has 8 ✏️.

Brain has 5 ✏️.

How many more does Pinky have than Brain?

$$\begin{array}{r} 8 \\ -\ 5 \\ \hline \end{array}$$

There is 1 🐟.

Then 5 more 🐟 come.

Now how many in all?

$$\begin{array}{r} 1 \\ +\ 5 \\ \hline \end{array}$$

23

ADDITION AND SUBTRACTION

Add or subtract. **STOP!** Watch the + and −.

2 + 5	8 − 3	7 + 0	8 − 4	6 + 1	7 − 2
7 − 5	3 + 3	4 + 2	0 + 6	8 − 0	8 − 6
8 − 1	7 − 1	1 + 6	6 − 5	3 + 4	5 + 1
6 − 6	2 + 4	5 + 2	6 − 0	1 + 7	7 − 3
1 + 5	6 − 3	7 − 4	4 + 3	8 − 2	4 + 4
7 − 6	5 + 3	6 − 2	0 + 8	2 + 6	8 − 8

PROBLEM SOLVING

Solve each problem.

There are 8 .

Then 7 ran away.

How many are left?

$$\begin{array}{r} 8 \\ -\ 7 \\ \hline \end{array}$$

There are 4 white .

There are 3 blue .

How many in all?

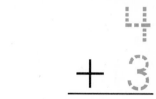

$$\begin{array}{r} 4 \\ +\ 3 \\ \hline \end{array}$$

Jon saw 7 taking off.

He saw 1 landing.

How many did he see in all?

Spencer has 6 .

He gave Morgan 4 .

How many does he have left?

There are 7 .

7 of the were eaten.

How many are left?

ADDITION AND SUBTRACTION

Add or subtract.
If you get 6, color
that part blue.

$\begin{array}{r} 6 \\ -4 \\ \hline \end{array}$

$\begin{array}{r} 8 \\ -3 \\ \hline \end{array}$

$7 - 4 =$

$\begin{array}{r} 2 \\ +5 \\ \hline \end{array}$

$\begin{array}{r} 8 \\ -4 \\ \hline \end{array}$

$2 + 3 =$

$4 + 1 =$

$0 + 8 =$

$2 + 4 =$

$\begin{array}{r} 2 \\ +1 \\ \hline \end{array}$

$0 + 6 =$

$1 + 5 =$

$\begin{array}{r} 5 \\ +1 \\ \hline \end{array}$

$2 + 4 =$

$\begin{array}{r} 0 \\ +6 \\ \hline \end{array}$

$\begin{array}{r} 7 \\ +2 \\ \hline \end{array}$

$4 + 2 =$

$\begin{array}{r} 8 \\ -4 \\ \hline \end{array}$

$7 - 1 =$

$\begin{array}{r} 7 \\ +1 \\ \hline \end{array}$

$6 - 0 =$

$\begin{array}{r} 2 \\ +2 \\ \hline \end{array}$

$3 + 3 =$

$1 + 5 =$

$\begin{array}{r} 7 \\ -7 \\ \hline \end{array}$

$\begin{array}{r} 7 \\ +0 \\ \hline \end{array}$

$\begin{array}{r} 8 \\ -7 \\ \hline \end{array}$

$\begin{array}{r} 0 \\ +8 \\ \hline \end{array}$

$\begin{array}{r} 6 \\ -6 \\ \hline \end{array}$

CHECKUP

Add.

3	0	4	2	2
+ 5	+ 6	+ 3	+ 5	+ 6

5	4	4	1	7
+ 1	+ 4	+ 2	+ 6	+ 1

Subtract.

6	7	8	6	8
− 4	− 2	− 6	− 3	− 0

8	7	6	6	8
− 1	− 5	− 2	− 0	− 3

Add or subtract. Watch the + and −.

3	6	7	3	8
+ 3	− 1	− 4	+ 4	− 7

7	5	8	7	6
− 7	+ 2	− 4	+ 0	+ 2

Sums of 9

Add.

$$\begin{array}{r} 2 \\ + 7 \\ \hline \end{array}$$

2 + 7 = 9

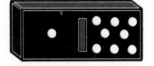
$$\begin{array}{r} 7 \\ + 2 \\ \hline \end{array}$$

7 + 2 =

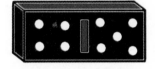
$$\begin{array}{r} 5 \\ + 4 \\ \hline \end{array}$$

5 + 4 =

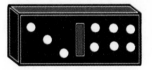
$$\begin{array}{r} 4 \\ + 5 \\ \hline \end{array}$$

4 + 5 =

$$\begin{array}{r} 1 \\ + 8 \\ \hline \end{array}$$

1 + 8 =

$$\begin{array}{r} 8 \\ + 1 \\ \hline \end{array}$$

8 + 1 =

$$\begin{array}{r} 3 \\ + 6 \\ \hline \end{array}$$

3 + 6 =

$$\begin{array}{r} 6 \\ + 3 \\ \hline \end{array}$$

6 + 3 =

$$\begin{array}{r} 0 \\ + 9 \\ \hline \end{array}$$

0 + 9 =

$$\begin{array}{r} 9 \\ + 0 \\ \hline \end{array}$$

9 + 0 =

$$\begin{array}{r} 5 \\ + 4 \\ \hline \end{array} \qquad \begin{array}{r} 3 \\ + 6 \\ \hline \end{array} \qquad \begin{array}{r} 8 \\ + 1 \\ \hline \end{array} \qquad \begin{array}{r} 4 \\ + 5 \\ \hline \end{array} \qquad \begin{array}{r} 7 \\ + 2 \\ \hline \end{array} \qquad \begin{array}{r} 0 \\ + 8 \\ \hline \end{array}$$

SUBTRACTING FROM 9

Subtract.

$$\begin{array}{r} 9 \\ -\ 6 \\ \hline \end{array}$$

$9 - 6 = $

$$\begin{array}{r} 9 \\ -\ 3 \\ \hline \end{array}$$

$9 - 3 = $

$$\begin{array}{r} 9 \\ -\ 0 \\ \hline \end{array}$$

$9 - 0 = $

$$\begin{array}{r} 9 \\ -\ 9 \\ \hline \end{array}$$

$9 - 9 = $

$$\begin{array}{r} 9 \\ -\ 5 \\ \hline \end{array}$$

$9 - 5 = $

$$\begin{array}{r} 9 \\ -\ 4 \\ \hline \end{array}$$

$9 - 4 = $

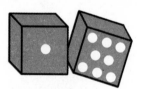
$$\begin{array}{r} 9 \\ -\ 8 \\ \hline \end{array}$$

$9 - 8 = $

$$\begin{array}{r} 9 \\ -\ 1 \\ \hline \end{array}$$

$9 - 1 = $

$$\begin{array}{r} 9 \\ -\ 2 \\ \hline \end{array}$$

$9 - 2 = $

$$\begin{array}{r} 9 \\ -\ 7 \\ \hline \end{array}$$

$9 - 7 = $

SUMS OF 10

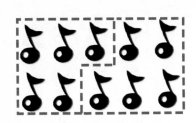

$$5 + 5 = 10$$

$$\begin{array}{r} 5 \\ + 5 \\ \hline 10 \end{array}$$

Add.

$$\begin{array}{r} 7 \\ + 3 \\ \hline 10 \end{array}$$

$$7 + 3 = 10$$

$$\begin{array}{r} 3 \\ + 7 \\ \hline \end{array}$$

$$3 + 7 = $$

$$1 + 9 = $$

$$\begin{array}{r} 1 \\ + 9 \\ \hline \end{array} \quad \begin{array}{r} 9 \\ + 1 \\ \hline \end{array}$$

$$2 + 8 = $$

$$\begin{array}{r} 2 \\ + 8 \\ \hline \end{array} \quad \begin{array}{r} 8 \\ + 2 \\ \hline \end{array}$$

$$9 + 1 = $$

$$8 + 2 = $$

$$6 + 4 = $$

$$\begin{array}{r} 6 \\ + 4 \\ \hline \end{array} \quad \begin{array}{r} 4 \\ + 6 \\ \hline \end{array}$$

$$10 + 0 = $$

$$\begin{array}{r} 10 \\ + 0 \\ \hline \end{array} \quad \begin{array}{r} 0 \\ + 10 \\ \hline \end{array}$$

$$4 + 6 = $$

$$0 + 10 = $$

$$\begin{array}{r} 3 \\ + 7 \\ \hline \end{array} \quad \begin{array}{r} 6 \\ + 2 \\ \hline \end{array} \quad \begin{array}{r} 5 \\ + 5 \\ \hline \end{array} \quad \begin{array}{r} 1 \\ + 9 \\ \hline \end{array} \quad \begin{array}{r} 2 \\ + 8 \\ \hline \end{array} \quad \begin{array}{r} 7 \\ + 2 \\ \hline \end{array}$$

SUBTRACTING FROM 10

$$\begin{array}{r} 10 \\ -\ 5 \\ \hline 5 \end{array}$$

$$10 - 5 = 5$$

$$\begin{array}{r} 10 \\ -\ 10 \\ \hline 0 \end{array}$$

$$10 - 10 = 0$$

Subtract.

$$\begin{array}{r} 10 \\ -\ 1 \\ \hline \end{array}$$

$$10 - 1 =$$

$$\begin{array}{r} 10 \\ -\ 9 \\ \hline \end{array}$$

$$10 - 9 =$$

$$10 - 7 =$$

$$\begin{array}{r} 10 \\ -\ 7 \\ \hline \end{array} \qquad \begin{array}{r} 10 \\ -\ 3 \\ \hline \end{array}$$

$$10 - 3 =$$

$$10 - 4 =$$

$$\begin{array}{r} 10 \\ -\ 4 \\ \hline \end{array} \qquad \begin{array}{r} 10 \\ -\ 6 \\ \hline \end{array}$$

$$10 - 6 =$$

$$10 - 8 =$$

$$\begin{array}{r} 10 \\ -\ 8 \\ \hline \end{array} \qquad \begin{array}{r} 10 \\ -\ 2 \\ \hline \end{array}$$

$$10 - 2 =$$

$$10 - 0 =$$

$$\begin{array}{r} 10 \\ -\ 0 \\ \hline \end{array}$$

$$\begin{array}{r} 10 \\ -\ 7 \\ \hline \end{array} \qquad \begin{array}{r} 10 \\ -\ 1 \\ \hline \end{array} \qquad \begin{array}{r} 10 \\ -\ 5 \\ \hline \end{array} \qquad \begin{array}{r} 10 \\ -\ 10 \\ \hline \end{array} \qquad \begin{array}{r} 10 \\ -\ 2 \\ \hline \end{array} \qquad \begin{array}{r} 10 \\ -\ 6 \\ \hline \end{array}$$

PRACTICING ADDITION

Add.

6 + 4	7 + 2	4 + 4	4 + 5	9 + 1	3 + 2
2 + 7	6 + 2	9 + 0	2 + 5	1 + 4	4 + 6
8 + 1	2 + 2	3 + 6	1 + 7	7 + 3	1 + 8
2 + 3	2 + 8	3 + 5	8 + 2	6 + 1	0 + 9
1 + 9	6 + 3	3 + 4	5 + 2	5 + 4	4 + 3
5 + 3	8 + 0	5 + 5	3 + 7	2 + 6	3 + 3

PROBLEM SOLVING

Solve each problem.

There are 5 white .

There are 4 blue .

How many in all?

$$\begin{array}{r} 5 \\ + 4 \\ \hline \end{array}$$

There are 3 .

7 more come.

How many are there now?

Pinky has 9 .

He buys 1 more.

Now how many does he have?

There are 6 .

There are 3 more .

How many in all?

There were 8 .

2 more came.

Then how many were there?

NAME _____

PRACTICING SUBTRACTION

Subtract.

9 − 4	7 − 6	10 − 5	9 − 7	8 − 5	10 − 9
10 − 4	6 − 3	9 − 6	10 − 3	9 − 0	5 − 1
3 − 1	9 − 1	10 − 8	7 − 2	9 − 5	2 − 2
10 − 1	7 − 0	5 − 3	8 − 7	10 − 2	6 − 4
9 − 8	7 − 4	10 − 0	4 − 2	8 − 4	9 − 3
10 − 6	8 − 6	9 − 2	8 − 1	9 − 9	10 − 7

PROBLEM SOLVING

Solve each problem.

There are 10 white .

There are 4 blue .

How many more white 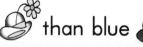 than blue 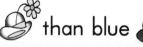?

$$\begin{array}{r} 10 \\ -\ 4 \\ \hline \end{array}$$

10 are on the table.

2 are broken.

How many are not broken?

There are 9 .

6 swim away.

How many are left?

Joni wants 9 .

She has 5 .

How many more does she need?

There were 10 .

5 melted.

How many did not melt?

ADDITION AND SUBTRACTION

Add or subtract. **STOP!** Watch the + and −.

5 + 2	10 − 6	7 + 1	9 − 4	1 + 9	9 − 8
9 + 0	8 − 0	10 − 9	1 + 8	2 + 7	9 − 1
10 − 1	2 + 8	1 + 6	8 − 3	6 + 3	10 − 3
9 − 9	4 + 5	8 + 1	10 − 8	9 − 0	5 + 5
4 + 4	9 − 3	7 + 3	9 − 7	3 + 6	10 − 7
7 + 2	8 − 7	0 + 8	9 − 2	10 − 5	4 + 6

PROBLEM SOLVING

Solve each problem.

There are 9 white .

There are 4 blue .

How many more white than blue ?

$$\begin{array}{r} 9 \\ -\ 4 \\ \hline \end{array}$$

Buttons has 7 .

He finds 2 more.

Now how many does he have?

$$\begin{array}{r} 7 \\ +\ 2 \\ \hline \end{array}$$

There are 5 .

There are 5 more .

How many in all?

There were 10 .

6 ran away.

Then how many were there?

There were 9 .

8 were eaten.

How many were not eaten?

TIME AND MEASUREMENT

Write the time for each clock.

7:30

thirty

_____ : _____

_____ : _____

Use an centimeter ruler.

How long is each object?

_____ centimeters

_____ centimeters

Use an inch ruler.

How long is each object?

_____ inches

_____ inch

_____ inches

ADDITION AND SUBTRACTION

Add.

5 + 2	7 + 1	3 + 7	2 + 2	6 + 3	3 + 2
1 + 8	3 + 1	1 + 1	2 + 8	3 + 4	5 + 4
2 + 1	5 + 5	9 + 1	2 + 6	4 + 4	10 + 0

Subtract.

8 − 1	9 − 9	6 − 3	7 − 0	4 − 2	10 − 3
10 − 9	9 − 6	7 − 6	10 − 8	5 − 4	9 − 2
5 − 3	8 − 5	10 − 6	6 − 4	9 − 8	7 − 4

ADDITION AND SUBTRACTION

Add or subtract.
If you get 5, color
that part green.

$$10 - 4$$

$$4 + 2$$

$$4 + 1$$

$$9 - 3$$

$$5 + 5$$

$$6 - 0$$

$$4 + 4 =$$

$$3 + 5$$

$$7 - 3 =$$

$$8 - 3$$

$$8 - 4$$

$$2 + 7$$

$$3 + 2$$

$$9 - 4$$

$$1 + 4$$

$$5 - 0$$

$$3 + 3$$

$$10 - 5$$

$$5 + 0$$

$$8 - 3$$

$$6 - 1$$

$$7 - 2$$

$$2 + 3$$

$$9 - 4$$

$$0 + 5$$

$$6 + 1$$

$$8 - 6$$

$$4 + 6$$

$$4 + 5$$

$$9 - 7 =$$

ADDING AND SUBTRACTING TENS

2 tens 20	8 tens 80
+ 6 tens + 60	− 6 tens − 60
8 tens 80	2 tens 20

Add.

4 tens   40
+ 5 tens   + 50

_____ tens

1 ten   10
+ 5 tens   + 50

_____ tens

30	80	60
+40	+10	+30

20	40	10
+30	+40	+70

50	60	30
+20	+10	+30

Subtract.

9 tens   90
− 5 tens   − 50

_____ tens

6 tens   60
− 5 tens   − 50

_____ ten

50	60	90
−40	−20	−30

20	90	30
−10	−70	−20

80	70	90
−30	−40	−60

41

PROBLEM SOLVING

Solve each problem.

There are 90 .

40 are used.

How many are not used?

$$90 - 40$$

You have 20 .

You buy 30 more.

Now how many do you have?

$$20 + 30$$

Tracy had 60 .

She spent 40 .

How many does she have left?

Charles found 10 .

Then he found 20 more.

Now how many does he have?

There were 80 .

60 ran away.

Then how many were there?

NAME

ADDITION
(2 DIGITS)

Join the pennies.
Add the ones.

Join the dimes.
Add the tens.

$$\begin{array}{r} 34 \\ +25 \\ \hline 9 \end{array}$$
→
$$\begin{array}{r} 34 \\ +25 \\ \hline 59 \end{array}$$

Add.

$$\begin{array}{r} 47 \\ +\ 2 \\ \hline 49 \end{array}$$
— Add the ones.
— Add the tens.

$$\begin{array}{r} 52 \\ +44 \\ \hline \end{array}$$
$$\begin{array}{r} 84 \\ +10 \\ \hline \end{array}$$
$$\begin{array}{r} 26 \\ +13 \\ \hline \end{array}$$

$$\begin{array}{r} 11 \\ +14 \\ \hline \end{array}$$
$$\begin{array}{r} 31 \\ +12 \\ \hline \end{array}$$
$$\begin{array}{r} 12 \\ +\ 1 \\ \hline \end{array}$$
$$\begin{array}{r} 78 \\ +11 \\ \hline \end{array}$$
$$\begin{array}{r} 43 \\ +10 \\ \hline \end{array}$$

$$\begin{array}{r} 50 \\ +18 \\ \hline \end{array}$$
$$\begin{array}{r} 18 \\ +50 \\ \hline \end{array}$$
$$\begin{array}{r} 81 \\ +\ 5 \\ \hline \end{array}$$
$$\begin{array}{r} 75 \\ +23 \\ \hline \end{array}$$
$$\begin{array}{r} 54 \\ +42 \\ \hline \end{array}$$

$$\begin{array}{r} 43 \\ +16 \\ \hline \end{array}$$
$$\begin{array}{r} 22 \\ +26 \\ \hline \end{array}$$
$$\begin{array}{r} 43 \\ +\ 2 \\ \hline \end{array}$$
$$\begin{array}{r} 33 \\ +54 \\ \hline \end{array}$$
$$\begin{array}{r} 31 \\ +26 \\ \hline \end{array}$$

PROBLEM SOLVING

Solve each problem.

$$\begin{array}{r} 24 \\ +\ 35 \\ \hline \end{array}$$

There are 24 .

35 more are planted.

Now how many are there?

Pinky had 27 .

He bought 12 more.

Now how many does he have?

Pinky has 54 .

Brain has 34 .

How many do they have in all?

You found 82 .

Then you find 7 more.

Now how many do you have?

---

20 are blue.

79 are white.

How many and are there in all?

ADDITION (2 DIGITS)

Add.

24 +13 37	75 + 4 79	50 +27	62 +15	46 +23
52 +34	96 + 2	73 +16	38 +40	35 +21
10 +21	14 + 5	12 +34	33 +53	13 +11
24 +21	57 + 2	60 +33	12 +43	71 +26
16 +52	28 + 1	51 +27	40 +45	63 +16

45

20¢   32¢   15¢   43¢

Solve each problem.

You buy a  and a .   20¢ + 15¢

You spent ____ ¢

You buy a and a .   15¢ + 32¢

You spent ____ ¢

You buy a and a .   ____ + ____ ¢

You spent ____ ¢

You buy a and a .   ____ + ____ ¢

You spent ____ ¢

You buy a and a .   ____ + ____ ¢

You spent ____ ¢

You buy a and a .   ____ + ____ ¢

You spent ____ ¢

46

SUBTRACTION (2 DIGITS)

Take away 4 pennies.
Subtract the ones.

$$\begin{array}{r} 36 \\ -24 \\ \hline 2 \end{array}$$

→

Take away 2 dimes.
Subtract the tens.

$$\begin{array}{r} 36 \\ -24 \\ \hline 12 \end{array}$$

Subtract.

$$\begin{array}{r} 78 \\ -\ 6 \\ \hline 72 \end{array}$$

↑ ↑ ——Subtract the ones.
——Subtract the tens.

$$\begin{array}{r} 69 \\ -47 \\ \hline \end{array}$$

$$\begin{array}{r} 28 \\ -15 \\ \hline \end{array}$$

$$\begin{array}{r} 45 \\ -32 \\ \hline \end{array}$$

$$\begin{array}{r} 59 \\ -45 \\ \hline \end{array}$$

$$\begin{array}{r} 98 \\ -43 \\ \hline \end{array}$$

$$\begin{array}{r} 17 \\ -\ 5 \\ \hline \end{array}$$

$$\begin{array}{r} 57 \\ -43 \\ \hline \end{array}$$

$$\begin{array}{r} 48 \\ -34 \\ \hline \end{array}$$

$$\begin{array}{r} 58 \\ -17 \\ \hline \end{array}$$

$$\begin{array}{r} 85 \\ -25 \\ \hline \end{array}$$

$$\begin{array}{r} 87 \\ -\ 7 \\ \hline \end{array}$$

$$\begin{array}{r} 96 \\ -80 \\ \hline \end{array}$$

$$\begin{array}{r} 66 \\ -51 \\ \hline \end{array}$$

$$\begin{array}{r} 94 \\ -41 \\ \hline \end{array}$$

$$\begin{array}{r} 39 \\ -22 \\ \hline \end{array}$$

$$\begin{array}{r} 33 \\ -\ 2 \\ \hline \end{array}$$

$$\begin{array}{r} 65 \\ -22 \\ \hline \end{array}$$

$$\begin{array}{r} 78 \\ -65 \\ \hline \end{array}$$

PROBLEM SOLVING

Solve each problem.

There are 54 🌹.

32 were picked.

How many are left?

54
− 32

You have 48 boxes.

35 📦 are blue.

The rest are white 📦.

How many white ones are there?

A store has 99 🍭.

The store sold 73.

How many 🍭 does the store have now?

Ellie has 23 📄.

Tom has 12 📄.

How many more 📄 does Ellie have?

To build a 🏠 you need 48 🔩.

You have 28 🔩.

How many more 🔩 do you need?

SUBTRACTION
(2 DIGITS)

Subtract.

75 − 34 **41**	67 − 4 *63*	30 − 20	48 − 30	55 − 32
78 − 67	56 − 3	98 − 86	86 − 15	98 − 48
95 − 31	84 − 2	65 − 45	79 − 48	84 − 50
42 − 10	39 − 6	89 − 42	67 − 21	66 − 36
98 − 73	72 − 2	43 − 13	57 − 32	69 − 15

PROBLEM SOLVING

59¢   15¢   42¢   30¢

Solve each problem.

You have   6 2¢
You buy a   — 42¢
You have left   20¢

You have   5 0¢
You buy a   — 30¢
You have left   ¢

You have   5 3¢
You buy a —   ¢
You have left   ¢

You have   9 9¢
You buy a —   ¢
You have left   ¢

You have   7 6¢
You buy a —   ¢
You have left   ¢

You have   4 5¢
You buy a —   ¢
You have left   ¢

ADDING 3 NUMBERS

Add the ones.

```
  1 2
  5 3  ⟶  5
+ 2 4     + 4
          ___
    9
```

⟶

Add the tens.

```
         1 2
  6 0    5 3
+ 2 0  + 2 4
_____    ___
         8 9
```

Add.

```
   4 5        3 2        3 5        4 7
   3 3        3 7        2 1        2 0
 + 1 0      + 2 0      + 1 1      + 2 2
 _____     _____     _____     _____
   8 8        8 9
```

— Add the ones.
— Add the tens.

```
   2 4        3 1        4 0        5 4        4 5
   2 4        2 3        1 3        1 0        3 3
 + 2 1      + 3 1      + 1 1      + 2 3      + 1 0
 _____     _____     _____     _____     _____
```

```
   6 1        3 0        3 6        3 1        4 4
   1 2        2 4        3 2        2 0        2 0
 + 2 4      + 1 5      + 3 1      + 2 4      + 3 4
 _____     _____     _____     _____     _____
```

PROBLEM SOLVING

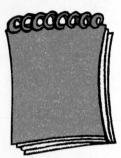   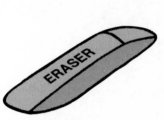

31¢   25¢   11¢   23¢

Solve each problem.

You buy a ✏,   11 ¢

an ▬,   23 ¢

and a 📓. + 31 ¢

You spent _____ ¢

You buy a 📓,   ___ ¢

a ✒,   ___ ¢

and a ✏. + _____ ¢

You spent _____ ¢

You buy an ▬,   ___ ¢

a 📓,   ___ ¢

and a ✒. + _____ ¢

You spent _____ ¢

You buy a ✒,   ___ ¢

a ✏,   ___ ¢

and an ▬. + _____ ¢

You spent _____ ¢

ADDITION AND SUBTRACTION

Add or subtract. **STOP!** Watch the + and −!

32 + 34	57 − 25	82 − 2	92 − 61	42 + 57
86 − 52	15 + 62	40 + 7	31 + 15	73 − 13
69 + 30	34 − 12	87 − 6	84 + 14	40 + 35
95 − 25	86 − 43	77 + 2	61 + 17	59 − 44
39 + 60	68 − 67	55 + 4	88 − 83	96 − 81

PROBLEM SOLVING

Solve each problem.

There are 45 blue ⬤ .

There are 43 white ⚪ .

How many more blue ⬤ than white ⚪ ?

$$\begin{array}{r} 45 \\ -\ 43 \\ \hline \end{array}$$

There are 19 🦅 .

30 more come.

How many are there now?

---

34 🥛 are on the table.

2 are broken.

How many are not broken?

You need 19 📎 .

You have 7 📎 .

How many more do you need?

You have 32 🪙 .

You get 57 more.

Now how many do you have?

ADDITION AND SUBTRACTION

Add or subtract. STOP! Watch the + and −!
If you get 56, color that part blue.

22 + 34 **56**	78 − 24	59 − 3	75 − 11	15 + 41
96 − 40	15 + 62	50 + 6	61 + 15	67 − 11
69 − 13	78 − 22	57 − 1	84 + 14	40 + 16
97 − 41	86 − 32	54 + 2	61 + 17	99 − 43
31 + 25	68 − 67	52 + 4	88 − 83	79 − 23

CHECKUP

Add.

30 + 50	34 + 5	61 + 24	18 + 31	50 + 36
45 + 21	92 + 7	73 + 13	54 + 24	82 + 17
35 + 12	60 + 8	30 40 + 10	51 16 + 12	26 21 + 12

Subtract.

70 − 40	85 − 2	54 − 30	97 − 35	74 − 54
28 − 18	78 − 4	46 − 23	89 − 33	93 − 62

NAME _____

FACTS FOR 11

Add or subtract.

$$\begin{array}{r} 8 \\ + 3 \\ \hline 11 \end{array}$$

$$\begin{array}{r} 3 \\ + 8 \\ \hline \end{array}$$

$$\begin{array}{r} 11 \\ - 8 \\ \hline 3 \end{array}$$

$$\begin{array}{r} 11 \\ - 3 \\ \hline \end{array}$$

$$\begin{array}{r} 9 \\ + 2 \\ \hline \end{array}$$

$$\begin{array}{r} 2 \\ + 9 \\ \hline \end{array}$$

$$\begin{array}{r} 11 \\ - 9 \\ \hline \end{array}$$

$$\begin{array}{r} 11 \\ - 2 \\ \hline \end{array}$$

$$\begin{array}{r} 6 \\ + 5 \\ \hline \end{array}$$

$$\begin{array}{r} 5 \\ + 6 \\ \hline \end{array}$$

$$\begin{array}{r} 11 \\ - 6 \\ \hline \end{array}$$

$$\begin{array}{r} 11 \\ - 5 \\ \hline \end{array}$$

$$\begin{array}{r} 7 \\ + 4 \\ \hline \end{array}$$

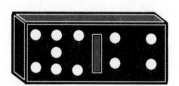

$$\begin{array}{r} 4 \\ + 7 \\ \hline \end{array}$$

$$\begin{array}{r} 11 \\ - 7 \\ \hline \end{array}$$

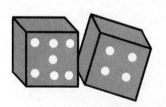

$$\begin{array}{r} 11 \\ - 4 \\ \hline \end{array}$$

$$\begin{array}{r} 7 \\ + 4 \\ \hline \end{array} \qquad \begin{array}{r} 6 \\ + 5 \\ \hline \end{array} \qquad \begin{array}{r} 3 \\ + 8 \\ \hline \end{array}$$

$$\begin{array}{r} 11 \\ + 0 \\ \hline \end{array} \qquad \begin{array}{r} 9 \\ + 2 \\ \hline \end{array} \qquad \begin{array}{r} 5 \\ + 6 \\ \hline \end{array}$$

$$\begin{array}{r} 11 \\ - 6 \\ \hline \end{array} \qquad \begin{array}{r} 11 \\ - 9 \\ \hline \end{array} \qquad \begin{array}{r} 11 \\ - 7 \\ \hline \end{array}$$

$$\begin{array}{r} 11 \\ - 2 \\ \hline \end{array} \qquad \begin{array}{r} 11 \\ - 0 \\ \hline \end{array} \qquad \begin{array}{r} 11 \\ - 8 \\ \hline \end{array}$$

57

PROBLEM SOLVING

Solve each problem.

   crayons in a box

$+$ 3   more crayons

_____

crayons in all

   _____ birds on a wire

$+$ _____ birds coming

_____

_____ birds in all

    blue hats

$+$ _____ black hats

_____

_____ hats in all

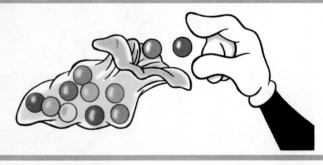   _____ marbles in a bag

$+$ _____ marbles are put in

_____

_____ marbles in all

    ants on a hill

$+$ _____ ants coming

_____

_____ ants in all

FACTS FOR 12

Add or subtract.

$$\begin{array}{r} 8 \\ + 4 \\ \hline 12 \end{array}$$

$$\begin{array}{r} 4 \\ + 8 \\ \hline \end{array}$$

$$\begin{array}{r} 12 \\ - 8 \\ \hline 4 \end{array}$$

$$\begin{array}{r} 12 \\ - 4 \\ \hline \end{array}$$

$$\begin{array}{r} 9 \\ + 3 \\ \hline \end{array}$$
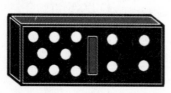
$$\begin{array}{r} 3 \\ + 9 \\ \hline \end{array}$$

$$\begin{array}{r} 12 \\ - 9 \\ \hline \end{array}$$

$$\begin{array}{r} 12 \\ - 3 \\ \hline \end{array}$$

$$\begin{array}{r} 7 \\ + 5 \\ \hline \end{array}$$

$$\begin{array}{r} 5 \\ + 7 \\ \hline \end{array}$$

$$\begin{array}{r} 12 \\ - 7 \\ \hline \end{array}$$

$$\begin{array}{r} 12 \\ - 5 \\ \hline \end{array}$$

$$\begin{array}{r} 6 \\ + 6 \\ \hline \end{array}$$
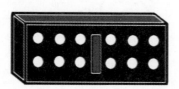

$$\begin{array}{r} 12 \\ - 6 \\ \hline \end{array}$$

$$\begin{array}{r} 9 \\ + 3 \\ \hline \end{array}\quad\begin{array}{r} 5 \\ + 7 \\ \hline \end{array}\quad\begin{array}{r} 12 \\ + 0 \\ \hline \end{array}$$

$$\begin{array}{r} 12 \\ - 6 \\ \hline \end{array}\quad\begin{array}{r} 12 \\ - 0 \\ \hline \end{array}\quad\begin{array}{r} 12 \\ - 8 \\ \hline \end{array}$$

$$\begin{array}{r} 6 \\ + 6 \\ \hline \end{array}\quad\begin{array}{r} 4 \\ + 8 \\ \hline \end{array}\quad\begin{array}{r} 7 \\ + 5 \\ \hline \end{array}$$

$$\begin{array}{r} 12 \\ - 5 \\ \hline \end{array}\quad\begin{array}{r} 12 \\ - 9 \\ \hline \end{array}\quad\begin{array}{r} 12 \\ - 4 \\ \hline \end{array}$$

 59

PROBLEM SOLVING

Solve each problem.

12   birds in all

— 4   birds flying away

_____ birds stay

_____ cars in all

— _____ cars leaving

_____ cars stay

_____ flowers in all

— _____ white flowers

_____ blue flowers

_____ buttons in all

— _____ black buttons

_____ blue buttons

_____ berries in all

— _____ berries falling

_____ berries not falling

FACTS THROUGH 12

Add.

8	7	6	3	9	6
+4	+4	+6	+9	+2	+5
12					

5	7	9	4	5	3
+5	+5	+1	+8	+7	+8

4	2	8	4	9	5
+6	+9	+3	+7	+3	+6

Subtract.

12	11	12	11	12	11
−8	−9	−5	−4	−6	−0
4					

12	12	10	11	10	11
−3	−7	−3	−8	−6	−5

12	11	10	12	11	12
−0	−2	−8	−4	−7	−9

PROBLEM SOLVING

Solve each problem.

_____ books on top shelf

+ _____ books on bottom shelf

_____ books in all

_____ cars in all

− _____ cars going

_____ cars parked

_____ eggs in the carton

+ _____ eggs on the table

_____ eggs in all

_____ crayons in all

− _____ crayons in the box

_____ crayons not in the box

_____ blue football helmets

+ _____ gray football helmets

_____ helmets in all

Add or subtract.

$$\begin{array}{r} 7 \\ + 6 \\ \hline 13 \end{array}$$

$$\begin{array}{r} 6 \\ + 7 \\ \hline \end{array}$$

$$\begin{array}{r} 13 \\ - 7 \\ \hline 6 \end{array}$$

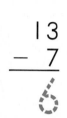

$$\begin{array}{r} 13 \\ - 6 \\ \hline \end{array}$$

$$\begin{array}{r} 8 \\ + 5 \\ \hline \end{array}$$

$$\begin{array}{r} 5 \\ + 8 \\ \hline \end{array}$$

$$\begin{array}{r} 13 \\ - 8 \\ \hline \end{array}$$

$$\begin{array}{r} 13 \\ - 5 \\ \hline \end{array}$$

$$\begin{array}{r} 9 \\ + 4 \\ \hline \end{array}$$

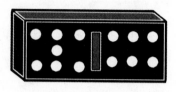

$$\begin{array}{r} 4 \\ + 9 \\ \hline \end{array}$$

$$\begin{array}{r} 13 \\ - 9 \\ \hline \end{array}$$

$$\begin{array}{r} 13 \\ - 4 \\ \hline \end{array}$$

$$\begin{array}{r} 5 \\ + 8 \\ \hline \end{array}$$
$$\begin{array}{r} 9 \\ + 4 \\ \hline \end{array}$$
$$\begin{array}{r} 7 \\ + 6 \\ \hline \end{array}$$

$$\begin{array}{r} 13 \\ - 5 \\ \hline \end{array}$$
$$\begin{array}{r} 13 \\ - 7 \\ \hline \end{array}$$
$$\begin{array}{r} 13 \\ - 9 \\ \hline \end{array}$$

$$\begin{array}{r} 6 \\ + 7 \\ \hline \end{array}$$
$$\begin{array}{r} 8 \\ + 5 \\ \hline \end{array}$$
$$\begin{array}{r} 4 \\ + 9 \\ \hline \end{array}$$

$$\begin{array}{r} 13 \\ - 4 \\ \hline \end{array}$$
$$\begin{array}{r} 13 \\ - 8 \\ \hline \end{array}$$
$$\begin{array}{r} 13 \\ - 6 \\ \hline \end{array}$$

NAME _____

FACTS FOR 14

<table>
</table>

Add or subtract.

$$\begin{array}{r} 9 \\ + 5 \\ \hline 14 \end{array}$$  $$\begin{array}{r} 5 \\ + 9 \\ \hline \end{array}$$ $$\begin{array}{r} 14 \\ - 9 \\ \hline 5 \end{array}$$  $$\begin{array}{r} 14 \\ - 5 \\ \hline \end{array}$$

$$\begin{array}{r} 8 \\ + 6 \\ \hline \end{array}$$  $$\begin{array}{r} 6 \\ + 8 \\ \hline \end{array}$$ $$\begin{array}{r} 14 \\ - 8 \\ \hline \end{array}$$  $$\begin{array}{r} 14 \\ - 6 \\ \hline \end{array}$$

$$\begin{array}{r} 7 \\ + 7 \\ \hline \end{array}$$ 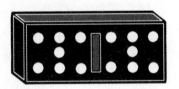 $$\begin{array}{r} 14 \\ - 7 \\ \hline \end{array}$$

$\begin{array}{r}8\\+6\\\hline\end{array}$	$\begin{array}{r}7\\+7\\\hline\end{array}$	$\begin{array}{r}6\\+6\\\hline\end{array}$	$\begin{array}{r}14\\-8\\\hline\end{array}$	$\begin{array}{r}12\\-7\\\hline\end{array}$	$\begin{array}{r}14\\-5\\\hline\end{array}$
$\begin{array}{r}9\\+4\\\hline\end{array}$	$\begin{array}{r}5\\+9\\\hline\end{array}$	$\begin{array}{r}7\\+4\\\hline\end{array}$	$\begin{array}{r}14\\-7\\\hline\end{array}$	$\begin{array}{r}13\\-8\\\hline\end{array}$	$\begin{array}{r}14\\-6\\\hline\end{array}$
$\begin{array}{r}9\\+5\\\hline\end{array}$	$\begin{array}{r}6\\+7\\\hline\end{array}$	$\begin{array}{r}6\\+8\\\hline\end{array}$	$\begin{array}{r}11\\-8\\\hline\end{array}$	$\begin{array}{r}14\\-9\\\hline\end{array}$	$\begin{array}{r}12\\-4\\\hline\end{array}$

ANSWER KEY

NUMBERS 0 TO 3

| zero 0 | one 1 | two 2 | three 3 |

Circle the number.

0 1 (2) 3	0 (1) 2 3
0 1 2 (3)	0 1 (2) 3
0 1 2 (3)	0 (1) 2 3

3

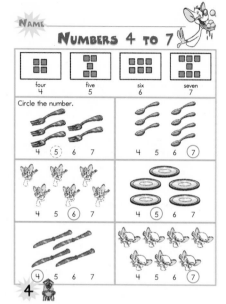

NUMBERS 4 TO 7

| four 4 | five 5 | six 6 | seven 7 |

Circle the number.

4 (5) 6 7	4 5 6 (7)
4 5 (6) 7	4 (5) 6 7
(4) 5 6 7	4 5 6 (7)

4

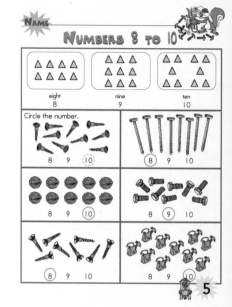

NUMBERS 8 TO 10

| eight 8 | nine 9 | ten 10 |

Circle the number.

8 9 (10)	(8) 9 10
8 9 (10)	8 (9) 10
(8) 9 10	8 9 (10)

5

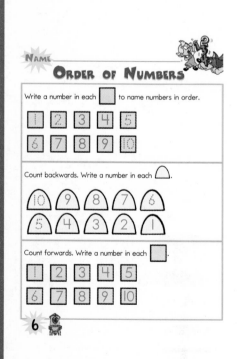

ORDER OF NUMBERS

Write a number in each ☐ to name numbers in order.

| 1 | 2 | 3 | 4 | 5 |
| 6 | 7 | 8 | 9 | 10 |

Count backwards. Write a number in each ⌒.

| 10 | 9 | 8 | 7 | 6 |
| 5 | 4 | 3 | 2 | 1 |

Count forwards. Write a number in each ☐.

| 1 | 2 | 3 | 4 | 5 |
| 6 | 7 | 8 | 9 | 10 |

6

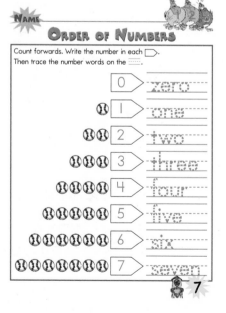

ORDER OF NUMBERS

Count forwards. Write the number in each ▷.
Then trace the number words on the ⁓.

0	zero
1	one
2	two
3	three
4	four
5	five
6	six
7	seven

7

ORDER OF NUMBERS

Connect the dots in order from 0 to 10.

8

65

ANSWER KEY

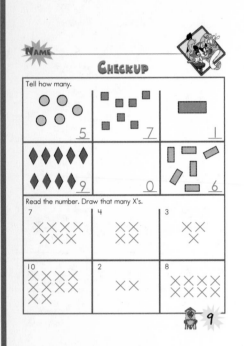

CHECKUP

Tell how many.

○ ○ ○ ○ ○ 5	▪ ▪ ▪ ▪ ▪ ▪ 7	▭ 1
◆ ◆ ◆ ◆ ◆ ◆ 9	0	▭ ▭ ▭ ▭ ▭ 6

Read the number. Draw that many X's.

7	4	3
XXXX XXX	XX XX	XX X
10	2	8
XXXXX XXXXX	XX	XXXX XXXX

9

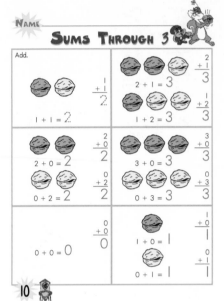

SUMS THROUGH 3

Add.

🥜 🥜 $\frac{+1}{2}$ $1 + 1 = 2$	🥜🥜🥜 $\frac{2}{+1}{3}$ $2 + 1 = 3$
	🥜🥜🥜 $\frac{2}{+1}{3}$ $1 + 2 = 3$
🥜🥜 $\frac{2}{+0}{2}$ $2 + 0 = 2$	🥜🥜🥜 $\frac{3}{+0}{3}$ $3 + 0 = 3$
🥜🥜 $\frac{0}{+2}{2}$ $0 + 2 = 2$	🥜🥜🥜 $\frac{0}{+3}{3}$ $0 + 3 = 3$
$\frac{0}{+0}{0}$ $0 + 0 = 0$	🥜 $\frac{1}{+0}{1}$ $1 + 0 = 1$ 🥜 $\frac{0}{+1}{1}$ $0 + 1 = 1$

10

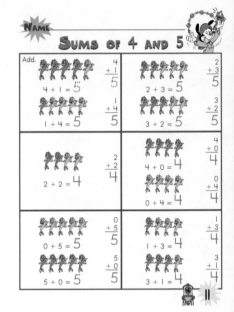

SUMS OF 4 AND 5

Add.

🐾🐾🐾🐾 $\frac{4}{+1}{5}$ $4 + 1 = 5$	🐾🐾 $\frac{2}{+3}{5}$ $2 + 3 = 5$
🐾🐾🐾🐾 $1 + 4 = 5$	🐾🐾 $\frac{3}{+2}{5}$ $3 + 2 = 5$
🐾🐾 $\frac{2}{+2}{4}$ $2 + 2 = 4$	🐾🐾🐾🐾 $\frac{4}{+0}{4}$ $4 + 0 = 4$ 🐾🐾🐾🐾 $\frac{0}{+4}{4}$ $0 + 4 = 4$
🐾🐾🐾🐾🐾 $\frac{0}{+5}{5}$ 🐾🐾🐾🐾🐾 $\frac{5}{+0}{5}$ $5 + 0 = 5$	🐾🐾🐾 $\frac{1}{+3}{4}$ 🐾🐾🐾 $\frac{3}{+1}{4}$ $3 + 1 = 4$

11

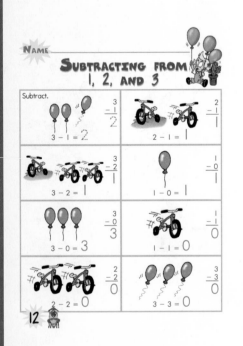

SUBTRACTING FROM 1, 2, AND 3

Subtract.

🎈🎈🎈 $\frac{3}{-1}{2}$ $3 - 1 = 2$	🚲🚲 $\frac{2}{-1}{1}$ $2 - 1 = 1$
🚲🚲🚲 $\frac{3}{-2}{1}$ $3 - 2 = 1$	🎈 $\frac{1}{-0}{1}$ $1 - 0 = 1$
🎈🎈🎈 $\frac{3}{-0}{3}$ $3 - 0 = 3$	🚲 $\frac{1}{-1}{0}$ $1 - 1 = 0$
🚲🚲 $\frac{2}{-2}{0}$ $2 - 2 = 0$	🎈🎈🎈 $\frac{3}{-3}{0}$ $3 - 3 = 0$

12

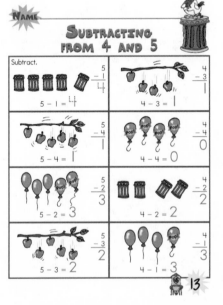

SUBTRACTING FROM 4 AND 5

Subtract.

🗑🗑🗑🗑🗑 $\frac{5}{-1}{4}$ $5 - 1 = 4$	🍎🍎🍎🍎 $\frac{4}{-3}{1}$ $4 - 3 = 1$
🍎🍎🍎🍎🍎 $\frac{5}{-4}{1}$ $5 - 4 = 1$	🎈🎈🎈🎈 $\frac{4}{-4}{0}$ $4 - 4 = 0$
🎈🎈🎈🎈🎈 $\frac{5}{-2}{3}$ $5 - 2 = 3$	🗑🗑🗑🗑 $\frac{4}{-2}{2}$ $4 - 2 = 2$
🍎🍎🍎🍎🍎 $\frac{5}{-3}{2}$ $5 - 3 = 2$	🎈🎈🎈🎈 $\frac{4}{-1}{3}$ $4 - 1 = 3$

13

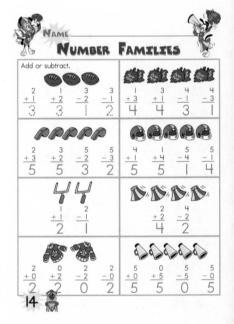

NUMBER FAMILIES

Add or subtract.

$\frac{2}{+1}{3}$	$\frac{1}{+2}{3}$	$\frac{3}{-2}{1}$	$\frac{3}{-1}{2}$	$\frac{1}{+3}{4}$	$\frac{3}{+1}{4}$	$\frac{4}{-1}{3}$	$\frac{4}{-3}{1}$
$\frac{2}{+3}{5}$	$\frac{3}{+2}{5}$	$\frac{5}{-2}{3}$	$\frac{5}{-3}{2}$	$\frac{4}{+1}{5}$	$\frac{1}{+4}{5}$	$\frac{5}{-1}{4}$	$\frac{5}{-4}{1}$
$\frac{1}{+1}{2}$	$\frac{2}{-1}{1}$			$\frac{2}{+2}{4}$	$\frac{4}{-2}{2}$		
$\frac{2}{+0}{2}$	$\frac{0}{+2}{2}$	$\frac{2}{-2}{0}$	$\frac{2}{-0}{2}$	$\frac{5}{+0}{5}$	$\frac{0}{+5}{5}$	$\frac{5}{-5}{0}$	$\frac{5}{-0}{5}$

14

66

ANSWER KEY

CHECKUP

Name

Add.

3 +1 = 4	1 +1 = 2	0 +0 = 0	2 +1 = 3	5 +0 = 5	1 +0 = 1
0 +3 = 3	2 +2 = 4	1 +2 = 3	0 +1 = 1	1 +4 = 5	3 +2 = 5
1 +3 = 4	4 +0 = 4	0 +5 = 5	2 +0 = 2	4 +1 = 5	2 +3 = 5

Subtract.

2 -1 = 1	4 -1 = 3	5 -0 = 5	3 -2 = 1	5 -4 = 1	4 -4 = 0
4 -0 = 4	5 -1 = 4	0 -0 = 0	4 -2 = 2	3 -0 = 3	5 -2 = 3
2 -0 = 2	4 -3 = 1	5 -3 = 2	3 -1 = 2	3 -3 = 0	1 -1 = 0

15

SUMS OF 6

Name

Add.

1 + 5 = 6 1 +5 = 6	2 + 4 = 6 2 +4 = 6
5 + 1 = 6 5 +1 = 6	4 + 2 = 6 4 +2 = 6
6 + 0 = 6 6 +0 = 6	3 + 3 = 6 3 +3 = 6
0 + 6 = 6 0 +6 = 6	

2 +4 = 6	1 +3 = 4	5 +1 = 6	3 +3 = 6	2 +2 = 4	3 +2 = 5

16

SUBTRACTING FROM 6

Name

Subtract.

6 - 1 = 5 6 -1 = 5	6 - 5 = 1 6 -5 = 1
6 - 4 = 2 6 -4 = 2	6 - 2 = 4 6 -2 = 4
6 - 3 = 3 6 -3 = 3	6 - 0 = 6 6 -0 = 6

6 -3 = 3	6 -6 = 0	6 -1 = 5	6 -4 = 2	6 -2 = 4	6 -5 = 1

17

SUMS OF 7

Name

Add.

3 + 4 = 7 3 +4 = 7	6 + 1 = 7 6 +1 = 7
4 + 3 = 7 4 +3 = 7	1 + 6 = 7 1 +6 = 7
7 + 0 = 7 7 +0 = 7	2 + 5 = 7 2 +5 = 7
0 + 7 = 7 0 +7 = 7	5 + 2 = 7 5 +2 = 7

5 +2 = 7	3 +3 = 6	4 +3 = 7	1 +6 = 7	3 +4 = 7	6 +0 = 6

18

SUBTRACTING FROM 7

Name

Subtract.

7 - 6 = 1 7 -6 = 1	7 - 1 = 6 7 -1 = 6
7 - 3 = 4 7 -3 = 4	7 - 4 = 3 7 -4 = 3
7 - 7 = 0 7 -7 = 0	7 - 0 = 7 7 -0 = 7
7 - 2 = 5 7 -2 = 5	7 - 5 = 2 7 -5 = 2

19

SUMS OF 8

Name

Add.

5 + 3 = 8 5 +3 = 8	7 + 1 = 8 7 +1 = 8
3 + 5 = 8 3 +5 = 8	1 + 7 = 8 1 +7 = 8
2 + 6 = 8 2 +6 = 8	4 + 4 = 8 4 +4 = 8
6 + 2 = 8 6 +2 = 8	

3 +3 = 6	5 +3 = 8	2 +6 = 8	8 +0 = 8	4 +3 = 7	0 +8 = 8

20

Subtracting from 8

Subtract.

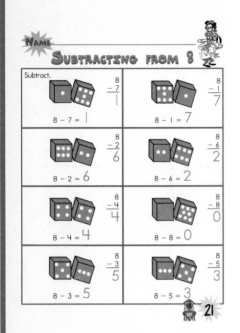

8 − 7 = 1	8 − 1 = 7
8 − 2 = 6	8 − 6 = 2
8 − 4 = 4	8 − 8 = 0
8 − 3 = 5	8 − 5 = 3

21

Addition and Subtraction

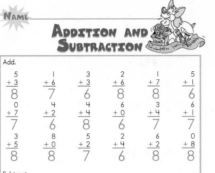

Add.

5 +3 = 8	1 +6 = 7	3 +4 = 7	2 +6 = 8	1 +7 = 8	5 +1 = 6
0 +7 = 7	4 +2 = 6	4 +4 = 8	6 +0 = 6	3 +4 = 7	6 +1 = 7
3 +5 = 8	8 +0 = 8	5 +2 = 7	2 +4 = 6	6 +2 = 8	0 +8 = 8

Subtract.

8 −3 = 5	6 −5 = 1	8 −4 = 4	7 −3 = 4	6 −2 = 4	6 −6 = 0
8 −1 = 7	7 −0 = 7	8 −1 = 7	8 −6 = 2	7 −1 = 6	8 −2 = 6
8 −8 = 0	6 −3 = 3	7 −1 = 6	8 −2 = 6	6 −1 = 5	7 −2 = 5

22

Problem Solving

Solve each problem.

There are 6 blue. There are 2 white. How many in all?	6 + 2 = 8
There are 7. 4 fly away. How many are left?	7 − 4 = 3
I saw 2 big. I saw 3 little. How many in all?	2 + 3 = 5
Pinky has 8. Brain has 5. How many more does Pinky have than Brain?	8 − 5 = 3
There is 1. Then 5 more come. Now how many in all?	1 + 5 = 6

23

Addition and Subtraction

Add or subtract. **STOP!** Watch the + and −.

2 +5 = 7	8 −3 = 5	7 +0 = 7	8 −4 = 4	6 +1 = 7	7 −2 = 5
7 −5 = 2	3 +3 = 6	4 +2 = 6	0 +6 = 6	8 −0 = 8	2 +6 = 8
8 −1 = 7	7 −1 = 6	1 +6 = 7	6 −5 = 1	3 +4 = 7	5 +1 = 6
6 −6 = 0	2 +4 = 6	5 +2 = 7	6 −0 = 6	1 +7 = 8	7 −3 = 4
1 +5 = 6	6 −3 = 3	7 −4 = 3	4 +3 = 7	8 −2 = 6	4 +4 = 8
7 −6 = 1	5 −1 = 4	6 −2 = 4	0 +8 = 8	2 +6 = 8	8 −8 = 0

24

Problem Solving

Solve each problem.

There are 8. Then 7 ran away. How many are left?	8 − 7 = 1
There are 4 white. There are 3 blue. How many in all?	4 + 3 = 7
Jon saw 7 taking off. He saw 1 landing. How many did he see in all?	7 + 1 = 8
Spencer has 6. He gave Morgan 4. How many does he have left?	6 − 4 = 2
There are 7. 7 of the were eaten. How many are left?	7 − 7 = 0

25

Addition and Subtraction

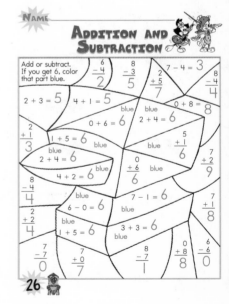

Add or subtract. If you get 6, color that part blue.

6 − 4 = 2 8 − 3 = 5 7 − 4 = 3 8 − 4 = 4

2 + 3 = 5   4 + 1 = 5   blue   blue   0 + 8 = 8

2 + 1 = 3   0 + 6 = 6   2 + 4 = 6

1 + 5 = 6 (blue)   blue   5 + 1 = 6

blue   2 + 4 = 6   0 + 6 = 6 (blue)   7 + 2 = 9

8 − 4 = 4   4 + 2 = 6   blue   7 − 1 = 6

2 + 2 = 4   6 − 0 = 6 (blue)   blue

blue   1 + 5 = 6   3 + 3 = 6 (blue)   blue

7 − 7 = 0   7 + 0 = 7   8 − 7 = 1   0 + 8 = 8   6 − 6 = 0

26

ANSWER KEY

CHECKUP

Name

Add.

3	0	4	2	2
+5	+6	+3	+5	+6
8	6	7	7	8

5	4	4	1	7
+1	+4	+2	+6	+1
6	8	6	7	8

Subtract.

6	7	8	6	8
−4	−2	−6	−3	−0
2	5	2	3	8

8	7	6	6	8
−1	−5	−2	−0	−3
7	2	4	6	5

Add or subtract. **STOP!** Watch the + and −.

3	6	7	3	8
+3	−1	−4	+4	−7
6	5	3	7	1

7	5	8	7	6
−7	+2	−4	+0	+2
0	7	4	7	8

27

SUMS OF 9

Name

Add.

2 + 7 = 9 | 2 / +7 / 9

5 + 4 = 9 | 5 / +4 / 9

7 + 2 = 9 | 7 / +2 / 9

4 + 5 = 9 | 4 / +5 / 9

1 + 8 = 9 | 1 / +8 / 9

3 + 6 = 9 | 3 / +6 / 9

8 + 1 = 9 | 8 / +1 / 9

6 + 3 = 9 | 6 / +3 / 9

0 + 9 = 9 | 0 / +9 / 9

9 + 0 = 9 | 9 / +0 / 9

5	3	8	4	7	0
+4	+6	+1	+5	+2	+8
9	9	9	9	9	8

28

SUBTRACTING FROM 9

Name

Subtract.

9 − 6 = 3 | 9 / −6 / 3

9 − 3 = 6 | 9 / −3 / 6

9 − 0 = 9 | 9 / −0 / 9

9 − 9 = 0 | 9 / −9 / 0

9 − 5 = 4 | 9 / −5 / 4

9 − 4 = 5 | 9 / −4 / 5

9 − 8 = 1 | 9 / −8 / 1

9 − 1 = 8 | 9 / −1 / 8

9 − 2 = 7 | 9 / −2 / 7

9 − 7 = 2 | 9 / −7 / 2

29

SUMS OF 10

Name

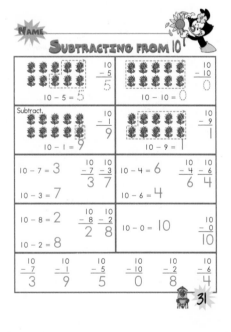

5 + 5 = 10 | 5 / +5 / 10

Add.

7 + 3 = 10 | 7 / +3 / 10

3 + 7 = 10 | 3 / +7 / 10

1 + 9 = 10 | 1 / +9 / 10   9 / +1 / 10

9 + 1 = 10

2 + 8 = 10 | 2 / +8 / 10   8 / +2 / 10

8 + 2 = 10

6 + 4 = 10 | 6 / +4 / 10   4 / +6 / 10

4 + 6 = 10

10 + 0 = 10 | 10 / +0 / 10   0 / +10 / 10

0 + 10 = 10

3	6	5	1	2	7
+7	+2	+5	+9	+8	+2
10	8	10	10	10	9

30

SUBTRACTING FROM 10

Name

10 − 5 = 5 | 10 / −5 / 5

10 − 10 = 0 | 10 / −10 / 0

Subtract.

10 − 1 = 9 | 10 / −1 / 9

10 − 9 = 1 | 10 / −9 / 1

10 − 7 = 3 | 10 / −7 / 3   10 / −3 / 7

10 − 3 = 7

10 − 4 = 6 | 10 / −4 / 6   10 / −6 / 4

10 − 6 = 4

10 − 8 = 2 | 10 / −8 / 2   10 / −2 / 8

10 − 2 = 8

10 − 0 = 10 | 10 / −0 / 10

10	10	10	10	10	10
−7	−1	−5	−10	−2	−6
3	9	5	0	8	4

31

PRACTICING ADDITION

Name

Add.

6	7	4	4	9	3
+4	+2	+4	+5	+1	+2
10	9	8	9	10	5

2	6	9	2	1	4
+7	+2	+0	+5	+4	+6
9	8	9	7	5	10

8	2	3	1	7	1
+1	+2	+6	+7	+3	+8
9	4	9	8	10	9

2	2	3	8	6	0
+3	+8	+5	+2	+1	+9
5	10	8	10	7	9

1	6	3	5	5	4
+9	+3	+4	+2	+4	+3
10	9	7	7	9	7

5	8	5	3	2	3
+3	+0	+5	+7	+6	+3
8	8	10	10	8	6

32

ANSWER KEY

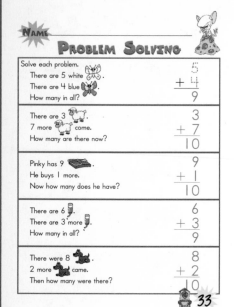

NAME _____

PROBLEM SOLVING

Solve each problem.

There are 5 white. There are 4 blue. How many in all?	5 + 4 9
There are 3. 7 more come. How many are there now?	3 + 7 10
Pinky has 9. He buys 1 more. Now how many does he have?	9 + 1 10
There are 6. There are 3 more. How many in all?	6 + 3 9
There were 8. 2 more came. Then how many were there?	8 + 2 10

33

NAME _____

PRACTICING SUBTRACTION

Subtract.

9 − 4 = 5	7 − 6 = 1	10 − 5 = 5	9 − 7 = 2	8 − 5 = 3	10 − 9 = 1
10 − 4 = 6	6 − 3 = 3	9 − 6 = 3	10 − 3 = 7	9 − 0 = 9	5 − 1 = 4
3 − 1 = 2	9 − 1 = 8	10 − 8 = 2	7 − 2 = 5	9 − 5 = 4	2 − 2 = 0
10 − 1 = 9	7 − 0 = 7	5 − 3 = 2	8 − 7 = 1	10 − 2 = 8	6 − 4 = 2
9 − 8 = 1	7 − 4 = 3	10 − 0 = 10	4 − 2 = 2	8 − 4 = 4	9 − 3 = 6
10 − 6 = 4	8 − 6 = 2	9 − 2 = 7	8 − 1 = 7	9 − 9 = 0	10 − 7 = 3

34

NAME _____

PROBLEM SOLVING

Solve each problem.

There are 10 white. There are 4 blue. How many more white than blue?	10 − 4 6
10 are on the table. 2 are broken. How many are not broken?	10 − 2 8
There are 9. 6 swim away. How many are left?	9 − 6 3
Joni wants 9. She has 5. How many more does she need?	9 − 5 4
There were 10. 5 melted. How many did not melt?	10 − 5 5

35

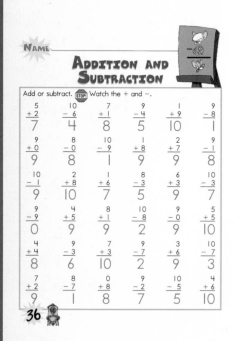

NAME _____

ADDITION AND SUBTRACTION

Add or subtract. **STOP** Watch the + and −.

5 + 2 = 7	10 − 6 = 4	7 + 1 = 8	9 − 4 = 5	1 + 9 = 10	9 − 8 = 1
9 + 0 = 9	8 − 0 = 8	10 − 9 = 1	1 + 8 = 9	2 + 7 = 9	9 − 1 = 8
10 − 1 = 9	2 + 8 = 10	1 + 6 = 7	8 − 3 = 5	6 + 3 = 9	10 − 3 = 7
9 − 9 = 0	4 + 5 = 9	8 + 1 = 9	10 − 8 = 2	9 − 0 = 9	5 + 5 = 10
4 + 4 = 8	9 − 3 = 6	7 + 3 = 10	9 − 7 = 2	3 + 6 = 9	10 − 7 = 3
7 + 2 = 9	8 − 7 = 1	0 + 8 = 8	9 − 2 = 7	10 − 5 = 5	4 + 6 = 10

36

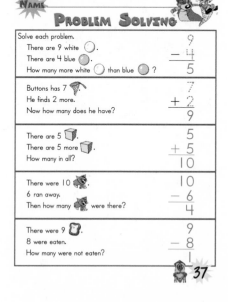

NAME _____

PROBLEM SOLVING

Solve each problem.

There are 9 white. There are 4 blue. How many more white than blue?	9 − 4 5
Buttons has 7. He finds 2 more. Now how many does he have?	7 + 2 9
There are 5. There are 5 more. How many in all?	5 + 5 10
There were 10. 6 ran away. Then how many were there?	10 − 6 4
There were 9. 8 were eaten. How many were not eaten?	9 − 8 1

37

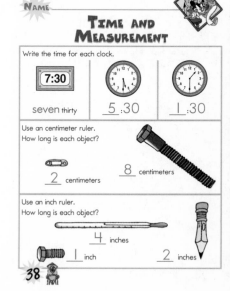

NAME _____

TIME AND MEASUREMENT

Write the time for each clock.

7:30		
seven thirty	5 :30	1 :30

Use an centimeter ruler. How long is each object?

2 centimeters   8 centimeters

Use an inch ruler. How long is each object?

4 inches   1 inch   2 inches

38

70

ANSWER KEY

NAME — ADDITION AND SUBTRACTION

Add.

5 +2 = 7	7 +1 = 8	3 +7 = 10	2 +2 = 4	6 +3 = 9	3 +2 = 5
1 +8 = 9	3 +1 = 4	1 +1 = 2	2 +8 = 10	3 +4 = 7	5 +4 = 9
2 +1 = 3	5 +5 = 10	9 +1 = 10	2 +6 = 8	4 +4 = 8	10 +0 = 10

Subtract.

8 -1 = 7	9 -9 = 0	6 -3 = 3	7 -0 = 7	4 -2 = 2	10 -3 = 7
10 -9 = 1	9 -6 = 3	3 -2 = 1	10 -8 = 2	5 -4 = 1	9 -2 = 7
5 -3 = 2	8 -5 = 3	10 -6 = 4	6 -4 = 2	9 -8 = 1	7 -4 = 3

39

NAME — ADDITION AND SUBTRACTION

Add or subtract.
If you get 5, color that part green.

10 - 4 = 6 ... green

4 +2 = 6

9 -3 = 6 ... 5 +1 = 6 ... 6 -0 = 6 ... 4 + 4 = 8 ... 8 -3 = 5 ... green

9 -4 = 5 green ... 2 +7 = 9 ... 3 +5 = 8 ... 8 -4 = 4

7 - 3 = 4

1 +4 = 5 green ... 10 -5 = 5 green ... 5 -0 = 5 green ... 5 +0 = 5 green ... 3 +3 = 6

9 -4 = 5 green ... 8 -3 = 5 green ... 6 -1 = 5 green

6 +1 = 7 ... 0 +5 = 5 green ... 7 -2 = 5 green ... 2 +3 = 5 green ... 5 -1 = 5 green ... 9 -4 = 5 green ... 4 +6 = 10

4 +5 = 9 green

9 - 7 = 2

40

NAME — ADDING AND SUBTRACTING TENS

2 tens +6 tens = 8 tens	20 +60 = 80	8 tens -6 tens = 2 tens	80 -60 = 20

Add.

4 tens +5 tens = 9 tens	40 +50 = 90
1 ten +5 tens = 6 tens	10 +50 = 60

Subtract.

9 tens -5 tens = 4 tens	90 -50 = 40
6 tens -5 tens = 1 ten	60 -50 = 10

30 +40 = 70	80 +10 = 90	60 +30 = 90	50 -40 = 10	60 -20 = 40	90 -30 = 60
20 +30 = 50	40 +40 = 80	10 +70 = 80	20 -10 = 10	90 -70 = 20	30 -20 = 10
50 +20 = 70	60 +10 = 70	30 +30 = 60	80 -30 = 50	70 -40 = 30	90 -60 = 30

41

NAME — PROBLEM SOLVING

Solve each problem.

There are 90. 40 are used. How many are not used?
90 - 40 = 50

You have 20. You buy 30 more. Now how many do you have?
20 + 30 = 50

Tracy had 60. She spent 40. How many does she have left?
60 - 40 = 20

Charles found 10. Then he found 20 more. Now how many does he have?
10 + 20 = 30

There were 80. 60 ran away. Then how many were there?
80 - 60 = 20

42

NAME — ADDITION (2 DIGITS)

Join the pennies. Add the ones.
34 +25 = 9 →

Join the dimes. Add the tens.
34 +25 = 59

Add.

47 + 2 = 49	52 +44 = 96	84 +10 = 94	26 +13 = 39
Add the ones. Add the tens.			

11 +14 = 25	31 +12 = 43	12 + 1 = 13	78 +11 = 89	43 +10 = 53
50 +18 = 68	18 +50 = 68	81 + 5 = 86	75 +23 = 98	54 +42 = 96
43 +16 = 59	22 +26 = 48	43 + 2 = 45	33 +54 = 87	31 +26 = 57

43

NAME — PROBLEM SOLVING

Solve each problem.

There are 24. 35 more are planted. Now how many are there?
24 + 35 = 59

Pinky had 27. He bought 12 more. Now how many does he have?
27 + 12 = 39

Pinky has 54. Brain has 34. How many do they have in all?
54 + 34 = 88

You found 82. Then you find 7 more. Now how many do you have?
82 + 7 = 89

20 are blue. 79 are white. How many blue and white are there in all?
20 + 79 = 99

44

71

ANSWER KEY

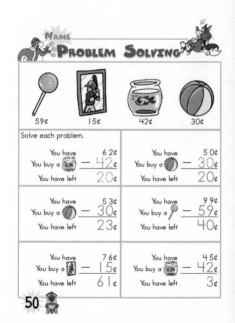

ADDITION (2 DIGITS)

Add.

24 +13 = 37	75 + 4 = 79	50 +27 = 77	62 +15 = 77	46 +23 = 69
52 +34 = 86	96 + 2 = 98	73 +16 = 89	38 +40 = 78	35 +21 = 56
10 +21 = 31	14 + 5 = 19	12 +34 = 46	33 +53 = 86	13 +11 = 24
24 +21 = 45	57 + 2 = 59	60 +33 = 93	12 +43 = 55	71 +26 = 97
16 +52 = 68	28 + 1 = 29	51 +27 = 78	40 +45 = 85	63 +16 = 79

45

PROBLEM SOLVING

20¢   32¢   15¢   43¢

Solve each problem.

You buy a (candle) and a (spool). + 20¢ + 15¢ = You spent 35¢

You buy a (spool) and a (needle). + 15¢ + 32¢ = You spent 47¢

You buy a (box) and a (spool). + 43¢ + 15¢ = You spent 58¢

You buy a (candle) and a (box). + 20¢ + 43¢ = You spent 63¢

You buy a (needle) and a (candle). + 32¢ + 20¢ = You spent 52¢

You buy a (box) and a (needle). + 43¢ + 32¢ = You spent 75¢

46

SUBTRACTION (2 DIGITS)

Take away 4 pennies. Subtract the ones. Take away 2 dimes. Subtract the tens.

36 − 24 = 2 → 36 − 24 = 12

Subtract.

78 − 6 = 72 (Subtract the ones. Subtract the tens.)		69 −47 = 22	28 −15 = 13	45 −32 = 13
59 −45 = 14	98 −43 = 55	17 − 5 = 12	57 −43 = 14	48 −34 = 14
58 −17 = 41	85 −25 = 60	87 − 7 = 80	96 −80 = 16	66 −51 = 15
94 −41 = 53	39 −22 = 17	33 − 2 = 31	65 −22 = 43	78 −65 = 13

47

PROBLEM SOLVING

Solve each problem.

There are 54 (bees).
32 were picked.
How many are left?
54 − 32 = 22

You have 48 boxes.
35 are blue.
The rest are white.
How many white ones are there?
48 − 35 = 13

A store has 99 (magnifiers).
The store sold 73.
How many does the store have now?
99 − 73 = 26

Ellie has 23 (cards).
Tom has 12 (cards).
How many more does Ellie have?
23 − 12 = 11

To build a (birdhouse) you need 48 (screws).
You have 28 (screws).
How many more do you need?
48 − 28 = 20

48

SUBTRACTION (2 DIGITS)

Subtract.

75 −34 = 41	67 − 4 = 63	30 −20 = 10	48 −30 = 18	55 −32 = 23
78 −67 = 11	56 − 3 = 53	98 −86 = 12	86 −15 = 71	98 −48 = 50
95 −31 = 64	84 − 2 = 82	65 −45 = 20	79 −48 = 31	84 −50 = 34
42 −10 = 32	39 − 6 = 33	89 −42 = 47	67 −21 = 46	66 −36 = 30
98 −73 = 25	72 − 2 = 70	43 −13 = 30	57 −32 = 25	69 −15 = 54

49

PROBLEM SOLVING

59¢   15¢   42¢   30¢

Solve each problem.

You have 62¢
You buy a (picture) − 42¢
You have left 20¢

You have 50¢
You buy a (ball) − 30¢
You have left 20¢

You have 53¢
You buy a (ball) − 30¢
You have left 23¢

You have 99¢
You buy a (lollipop) − 59¢
You have left 40¢

You have 76¢
You buy a (picture) − 15¢
You have left 61¢

You have 45¢
You buy a (picture) − 42¢
You have left 3¢

50

72

Answer Key

Name

Adding 3 Numbers

Add the ones.
```
 12      5
 53  →
+24    + 4
        9
```
Add the tens.
```
 60      12
+20      53
        +24
        +89
```

Add.

45 33 +10 = **88**	32 37 +20 = **89**	35 21 +11 = **67**	47 20 +22 = **89**

Add the ones.
Add the tens.

24 24 +21 = **69**	31 23 +31 = **85**	40 13 +11 = **64**	54 10 +23 = **87**	45 33 +10 = **88**
61 12 +24 = **97**	30 24 +15 = **69**	36 32 +31 = **99**	31 20 +24 = **75**	44 20 +34 = **98**

51

Name

Problem Solving

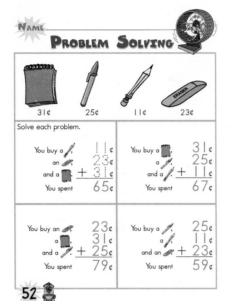

31¢   25¢   11¢   23¢

Solve each problem.

You buy a ✏, an ✎, and a 📒 + 31¢ = You spent **65¢**	You buy a 📒 25¢, and a ✏ + 11¢ = You spent **67¢**
You buy an ✎ 23¢, a 📒 31¢, and a ✏ + 25¢ = You spent **79¢**	You buy a ✏ 25¢, a ✎ 11¢, and an ✏ + 23¢ = You spent **59¢**

52

Name

Addition and Subtraction

Add or subtract. **STOP!** Watch the + and −!

32 +34 = **66**	57 −25 = **32**	82 − 2 = **80**	92 −61 = **31**	42 +57 = **99**
86 −52 = **34**	15 +62 = **77**	40 + 7 = **47**	31 +15 = **46**	73 −13 = **60**
69 +30 = **99**	34 −12 = **22**	87 − 6 = **81**	84 +14 = **98**	40 +35 = **75**
95 −25 = **70**	86 −43 = **43**	77 + 2 = **79**	61 +17 = **78**	59 −44 = **15**
39 +60 = **99**	68 −67 = **1**	55 + 4 = **59**	88 −83 = **5**	96 −81 = **15**

53

Name

Problem Solving

Solve each problem.

There are 45 blue ⚪.
There are 43 white ⚪.
How many more blue ⚪ than white ⚪?
```
 45
−43
  2
```

There are 19 🐞.
30 more come.
How many are there now?
```
 19
+30
 49
```

34 🥤 are on the table.
2 are broken.
How many are not broken?
```
 34
− 2
 32
```

You need 19 📎.
You have 7 📎.
How many more do you need?
```
 19
− 7
 12
```

You have 32 🪙.
You get 57 more.
Now how many do you have?
```
 32
+57
 89
```

54

Name

Addition and Subtraction

Add or subtract. **STOP!** Watch the + and −!
If you get 56, color that part blue.

22 +34 = **56** (blue)	78 −24 = **54**	blue 59 − 3 = **56**	75 −11 = **64**	blue 15 +41 = **56**
blue 96 −40 = **56**	15 +62 = **77**	blue 50 + 6 = **56**	61 +15 = **76**	blue 67 −11 = **56**
blue 69 −13 = **56**	blue 78 −22 = **56**	blue 57 − 1 = **56**	84 +14 = **98**	blue 40 +16 = **56**
blue 97 −41 = **56**	86 −32 = **54**	blue 54 + 2 = **56**	61 +17 = **78**	blue 99 −43 = **56**
blue 31 +25 = **56**	68 −67 = **1**	blue 52 + 4 = **56**	88 −83 = **5**	blue 79 −23 = **56**

55

Name

Checkup

Add.

30 +50 = **80**	34 + 5 = **39**	61 +24 = **85**	18 +31 = **49**	50 +36 = **86**
45 +21 = **66**	92 + 7 = **99**	73 +13 = **86**	54 +24 = **78**	82 +17 = **99**
35 +12 = **47**	60 + 8 = **68**	30 40 +10 = **80**	51 16 +12 = **79**	26 21 +12 = **59**

Subtract.

70 −40 = **30**	85 − 2 = **83**	54 −30 = **24**	97 −35 = **62**	74 −54 = **20**
28 −18 = **10**	78 − 4 = **74**	46 −23 = **23**	89 −33 = **56**	93 −62 = **31**

56

73

Answer Key

Name _____

Facts for 11

Add or subtract.

8 + 3 **11**	[domino]	3 + 8 **11**
9 + 2 **11**	[domino]	2 + 9 **11**
6 + 5 **11**	[domino]	5 + 6 **11**
7 + 4 **11**	[domino]	4 + 7 **11**

11 − 8 **3**	[dice]	11 − 3 **8**
11 − 9 **2**	[dice]	11 − 2 **9**
11 − 6 **5**	[dice]	11 − 5 **6**
11 − 7 **4**	[dice]	11 − 4 **7**

7 + 4 **11**	6 + 5 **11**	3 + 8 **11**	11 − 6 **5**	11 − 9 **2**	11 − 7 **4**
11 + 0 **11**	9 + 2 **11**	5 + 6 **11**	11 − 2 **9**	11 − 0 **11**	11 − 8 **3**

57

Name _____

Problem Solving

Solve each problem.

	8 + 3 **11**	crayons in a box more crayons crayons in all
[birds]	6 + 5 **11**	birds on a wire birds coming birds in all
[hats]	7 + 4 **11**	blue hats black hats hats in all
[marbles]	9 + 2 **11**	marbles in a bag marbles are put in marbles in all
[ants]	5 + 6 **11**	ants on a hill ants coming ants in all

58

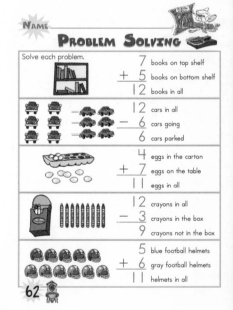

Name _____

Facts for 12

Add or subtract.

8 + 4 **12**	[domino]	4 + 8 **12**
9 + 3 **12**	[domino]	3 + 9 **12**
7 + 5 **12**	[domino]	5 + 7 **12**
6 + 6 **12**	[domino]	

12 − 4 **8**	[dice]	
12 − 9 **3**	[dice]	
12 − 7 **5**	[dice]	
12 − 6 **6**	[dice]	

9 + 3 **12**	5 + 7 **12**	12 + 0 **12**	12 − 6 **6**	12 − 0 **12**	12 − 8 **4**
6 + 6 **12**	4 + 8 **12**	7 + 5 **12**	12 − 5 **7**	12 − 9 **3**	12 − 4 **8**

59

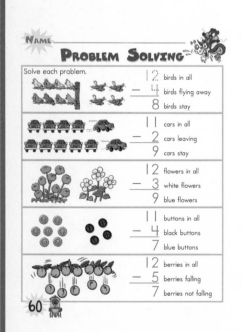

Name _____

Problem Solving

Solve each problem.

[birds]	12 − 4 **8**	birds in all birds flying away birds stay
[cars]	11 − 2 **9**	cars in all cars leaving cars stay
[flowers]	12 − 3 **9**	flowers in all white flowers blue flowers
[buttons]	11 − 4 **7**	buttons in all black buttons blue buttons
[berries]	12 − 5 **7**	berries in all berries falling berries not falling

60

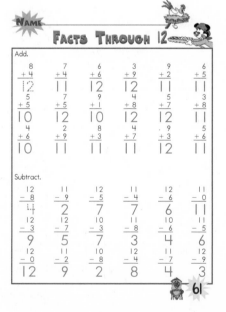

Name _____

Facts Through 12

Add.

8 + 4 **12**	7 + 4 **11**	6 + 6 **12**	3 + 9 **12**	9 + 2 **11**	6 + 5 **11**
5 + 5 **10**	7 + 5 **12**	9 + 1 **10**	4 + 8 **12**	5 + 7 **12**	3 + 8 **11**
4 + 6 **10**	2 + 9 **11**	8 + 3 **11**	4 + 7 **11**	9 + 3 **12**	5 + 6 **11**

Subtract.

12 − 8 **4**	11 − 9 **2**	12 − 5 **7**	11 − 4 **7**	12 − 6 **6**	11 − 0 **11**
12 − 3 **9**	12 − 7 **5**	10 − 3 **7**	11 − 8 **3**	10 − 6 **4**	11 − 5 **6**
12 − 0 **12**	11 − 2 **9**	10 − 8 **2**	12 − 4 **8**	11 − 7 **4**	12 − 9 **3**

61

Name _____

Problem Solving

Solve each problem.

[books]	7 + 5 **12**	books on top shelf books on bottom shelf books in all
[cars]	12 − 6 **6**	cars in all cars going cars parked
[eggs]	4 + 7 **11**	eggs in the carton eggs on the table eggs in all
[crayons]	12 − 3 **9**	crayons in all crayons in the box crayons not in the box
[helmets]	5 + 6 **11**	blue football helmets gray football helmets helmets in all

62

ANSWER KEY

FACTS FOR 13

Add or subtract.

7 + 6 = 13	6 + 7 = 13	13 − 7 = 6	13 − 6 = 7
8 + 5 = 13	5 + 8 = 13	13 − 8 = 5	13 − 5 = 8
9 + 4 = 13	4 + 9 = 13	13 − 9 = 4	13 − 4 = 9

5 + 8 = 13	9 + 4 = 13	7 + 6 = 13	13 − 5 = 8	13 − 7 = 6	13 − 9 = 4
6 + 7 = 13	8 + 5 = 13	4 + 9 = 13	13 − 4 = 9	13 − 8 = 5	13 − 6 = 7

63

FACTS FOR 14

Add or subtract.

9 + 5 = 14	5 + 9 = 14	14 − 9 = 5	14 − 5 = 9
8 + 6 = 14	6 + 8 = 14	14 − 8 = 6	14 − 6 = 8
7 + 7 = 14		14 − 7 = 7	

8 + 6 = 14	7 + 7 = 14	6 + 6 = 12	14 − 8 = 6	12 − 7 = 5	14 − 5 = 9
9 + 4 = 13	5 + 9 = 14	7 + 4 = 11	14 − 7 = 7	13 − 8 = 5	14 − 6 = 8
9 + 5 = 14	6 + 7 = 13	6 + 8 = 14	11 − 8 = 3	14 − 9 = 5	12 − 4 = 8

64

Look for all of these entertaining and educational titles in

The McGraw-Hill Junior Academic™ Workbook Series

Toddler

My Colors Go 'Round	ISBN 1-57768-208-4	UPC 6-09746-45118-5
My 1, 2, 3's	ISBN 1-57768-218-1	UPC 6-09746-45128-4
My A, B, C's	ISBN 1-57768-228-9	UPC 6-09746-45138-3
My Ups and Downs	ISBN 1-57768-238-6	UPC 6-09746-45148-2

Preschool

MATH	ISBN 1-57768-209-2	UPC 6-09746-45119-2
READING	ISBN 1-57768-219-X	UPC 6-09746-45129-1
VOWEL SOUNDS	ISBN 1-57768-229-7	UPC 6-09746-45139-0
SOUND PATTERNS	ISBN 1-57768-239-4	UPC 6-09746-45149-9

Kindergarten

MATH	ISBN 1-57768-200-9	UPC 6-09746-45110-9
READING	ISBN 1-57768-210-6	UPC 6-09746-45120-8
PHONICS	ISBN 1-57768-220-3	UPC 6-09746-45130-7
THINKING SKILLS	ISBN 1-57768-230-0	UPC 6-09746-45140-6

Grade 1

MATH	ISBN 1-57768-201-7	UPC 6-09746-45111-6
READING	ISBN 1-57768-211-4	UPC 6-09746-45121-5
PHONICS	ISBN 1-57768-221-1	UPC 6-09746-45131-4
WORD BUILDERS	ISBN 1-57768-231-9	UPC 6-09746-45141-3

Grade 2

MATH	ISBN 1-57768-202-5	UPC 6-09746-45112-3
READING	ISBN 1-57768-212-2	UPC 6-09746-45122-2
PHONICS	ISBN 1-57768-222-X	UPC 6-09746-45132-1
WORD BUILDERS	ISBN 1-57768-232-7	UPC 6-09746-45142-0

It's Serious Fun!!

The skills taught in school are now available at home! These titles are now available in retail stores and teacher supply stores everywhere. All titles meet school guidelines and are based on The McGraw-Hill Companies classroom software titles.

MATH GRADES 1 & 2

These math programs are a great way to teach and reinforce skills used in everyday situations. Fun, friendly characters need help with their math skills. Everyone's friend, Nubby the stubby pencil, will help kids master the math in the Numbers Quiz show. Foggy McHammer, a carpenter, needs some help building his playhouse so that all the boards will fit together! Julio Bambino's kitchen antics will surely burn his pastries if you don't help him set the clock timer correctly! We can't forget Turbo Tomato, a fruit with a passion for adventure, who needs help calculating his daredevil stunts.

   Math Grades 1 & 2 use a tested, proven approach to reinforcing your child's math skills while keeping him or her intrigued with Nubby and his collection of crazy friends.

TITLE	ISBN	PRICE
Grade 1: Nubby's Quiz Show	1-57768-011-1	$14.95
Grade 2: Foggy McHammer's Treehouse	1-57768-012-X	$14.95

MISSION MASTERS™ MATH AND LANGUAGE ARTS

The Mission Masters™—Pauline, Rakeem, Mia, and T.J.—need your help. The Mission Masters™ are a team of young agents working for the Intelliforce Agency, a high-level cooperative whose goal is to maintain order on our rather unruly planet. From within the agency's top secret Command Control Center, the agency's central computer, M5, has detected a threat...and guess what—you're the agent assigned to the mission!

MISSION MASTERS™ MATH GRADES 3, 4 & 5

This series of exciting activities encourages young mathematicians to challenge themselves and their math skills to overcome the perils of villains and other planetary threats. Skills reinforced include: analyzing and solving real-world problems, estimation, measurements, geometry, whole numbers, fractions, graphs, and patterns.

TITLE	ISBN	PRICE
Grade 3: Mission Masters™ Defeat Dirty D!	1-57768-013-8	$19.95
Grade 4: Mission Masters™ Alien Encounter	1-57768-014-6	$19.95
Grade 5: Mission Masters™ Meet Mudflat Moe	1-57768-015-4	$19.95

MISSION MASTERS™ LANGUAGE ARTS GRADES 3, 4 & 5

This series invites children to apply their language skills to defeat unscrupulous characters and to overcome other earthly dangers. Skills reinforced include: language mechanics and usage, punctuation, spelling, vocabulary, reading comprehension, and creative writing.

TITLE	ISBN	PRICE
Grade 3: Mission Masters™ Freezing Frenzy	1-57768-023-5	$24.95
Grade 4: Mission Masters™ Network Nightmare	1-57768-024-3	$24.95
Grade 5: Mission Masters™ Mummy Mysteries	1-57768-025-1	$24.95

Look for these and other exciting software titles at a retail store near you. All titles for Windows 3.1™, Windows '95™, and Macintosh™. Visit us on the Internet at

www.MHkids.com

Offers a selection of workbooks to meet all your needs.

Look for all of these fine educational workbooks
in the McGraw-Hill Learning Materials SPECTRUM Series.
All workbooks meet school curriculum guidelines and correspond to
The McGraw-Hill Companies classroom textbooks.

SPECTRUM SERIES

GEOGRAPHY

Full-color, three-part lessons strengthen geography knowledge and map reading skills. Focusing on five geographic themes including location, place, human/environmental interaction, movement, and regions. Over 150 pages. Glossary of geographical terms and answer key included.

TITLE	ISBN	PRICE
Grade 3, Communities	1-57768-153-3	$7.95
Grade 4, Regions	1-57768-154-1	$7.95
Grade 5, USA	1-57768-155-X	$7.95
Grade 6, World	1-57768-156-8	$7.95

MATH

Features easy-to-follow instructions that give students a clear path to success. This series has comprehensive coverage of the basic skills, helping children to master math fundamentals. Over 150 pages. Answer key included.

TITLE	ISBN	PRICE
Grade 1	1-57768-111-8	$6.95
Grade 2	1-57768-112-6	$6.95
Grade 3	1-57768-113-4	$6.95
Grade 4	1-57768-114-2	$6.95
Grade 5	1-57768-115-0	$6.95
Grade 6	1-57768-116-9	$6.95
Grade 7	1-57768-117-7	$6.95
Grade 8	1-57768-118-5	$6.95

PHONICS

Provides everything children need to build multiple skills in language. Focusing on phonics, structural analysis, and dictionary skills, this series also offers creative ideas for using phonics and word study skills in other language arts. Over 200 pages. Answer key included.

TITLE	ISBN	PRICE
Grade K	1-57768-120-7	$6.95
Grade 1	1-57768-121-5	$6.95
Grade 2	1-57768-122-3	$6.95
Grade 3	1-57768-123-1	$6.95
Grade 4	1-57768-124-X	$6.95
Grade 5	1-57768-125-8	$6.95
Grade 6	1-57768-126-6	$6.95

READING

This full-color series creates an enjoyable reading environment, even for below-average readers. Each book contains captivating content, colorful characters, and compelling illustrations, so children are eager to find out what happens next. Over 150 pages. Answer key included.

TITLE	ISBN	PRICE
Grade K	1-57768-130-4	$6.95
Grade 1	1-57768-131-2	$6.95
Grade 2	1-57768-132-0	$6.95
Grade 3	1-57768-133-9	$6.95
Grade 4	1-57768-134-7	$6.95
Grade 5	1-57768-135-5	$6.95
Grade 6	1-57768-136-3	$6.95

SPELLING

This full-color series links spelling to reading and writing and increases skills in words and meanings, consonant and vowel spellings, and proofreading practice. Over 200 pages. Speller dictionary and answer key included.

TITLE	ISBN	PRICE
Grade 1	1-57768-161-4	$7.95
Grade 2	1-57768-162-2	$7.95
Grade 3	1-57768-163-0	$7.95
Grade 4	1-57768-164-9	$7.95
Grade 5	1-57768-165-7	$7.95
Grade 6	1-57768-166-5	$7.95

WRITING

Lessons focus on creative and expository writing using clearly stated objectives and pre-writing exercises. Eight essential reading skills are applied. Activities include main idea, sequence, comparison, detail, fact and opinion, cause and effect, and making a point. Over 130 pages. Answer key included.

TITLE	ISBN	PRICE
Grade 1	1-57768-141-X	$6.95
Grade 2	1-57768-142-8	$6.95
Grade 3	1-57768-143-6	$6.95
Grade 4	1-57768-144-4	$6.95
Grade 5	1-57768-145-2	$6.95
Grade 6	1-57768-146-0	$6.95
Grade 7	1-57768-147-9	$6.95
Grade 8	1-57768-148-7	$6.95

TEST PREP from the Nation's #1 Testing Company

Prepares children to do their best on current editions of the five major standardized tests. Activities reinforce test-taking skills through examples, tips, practice, and timed exercises. Subjects include reading, math, and language. Over 150 pages. Answer key included.

TITLE	ISBN	PRICE
Grade 3	1-57768-103-7	$8.95
Grade 4	1-57768-104-5	$8.95
Grade 5	1-57768-105-3	$8.95
Grade 6	1-57768-106-1	$8.95
Grade 7	1-57768-107-X	$8.95
Grade 8	1-57768-108-8	$8.95